"*(Re)Generating Inclusive Cities* is an important and timely book. Dan Zuberi and Ariel Taylor examine the urban regeneration occurring in a number of American and Canadian cities as suburban expansion declines, and insightfully reveal how it heightens urban poverty and inequality. The authors also advance some thoughtful urban design recommendations to make these cities more socially just and inclusive. This book is a must-read for everyone concerned about the future of our cities."

**William Julius Wilson, Lewis P. and Linda L.**
*Geyser University Professor, Harvard University*

"From Zuberi and Taylor, we learn about the power (and problems) of mega projects like the High Line, the difficulties of brownfield reclamation, and the social and political challenges of mixed income housing. They challenge received wisdom about hyper-urbanization, force our attention to social policy differences that separate Canada and the US and hence inflect the unfolding of common pressures of globalization and neo-liberal policy making. It is a forceful, intelligent, empirically grounded work that all urban scholars will appreciate."

**Katherine Newman,** *Torrey Little Professor of Sociology and Provost University of Massachusetts, Amherst*

# (Re)Generating Inclusive Cities

As suburban expansion declines, cities have become essential economic, cultural and social hubs of global connectivity. This book is about urban revitalization across North America, in cities including San Francisco, Toronto, Boston, Vancouver, New York and Seattle. Infrastructure projects including the High Line and Big Dig are explored alongside urban neighborhood creation and regeneration projects such as Hunters Point in San Francisco and Regent Park in Toronto. Today, these urban regeneration projects have evolved in the context of unprecedented neoliberal public policy and soaring real estate prices. Consequently, they make a complex contribution to urban inequality and poverty trends in many of these cities, including the suburbanization of immigrant settlement and rising inequality.

*(Re)Generating Inclusive Cities* wrestles with challenging, but important questions of urban planning, including who benefits and who loses with these urban regeneration schemes, and what policy tools can be used to mitigate harm? We propose a new way forward for understanding and promoting better urban design practices in order to build more socially just and inclusive cities and to ultimately improve the quality of urban life for all.

**Dan Zuberi** is RBC Chair and Associate Professor of Social Policy at the Factor-Inwentash Faculty of Social Work and School of Public Policy and Governance at the University of Toronto, Canada. His research focuses on urban poverty, health, education, employment and social welfare.

**Ariel Taylor** is a PhD candidate in the Department of Political Science at the University of Victoria, Canada. Her research focuses on democratization, civil society, neoliberalism and private governance. She holds a Social Sciences and Humanities Research Council of Canada Graduate Fellowship.

## Routledge Research in Planning and Urban Design

Series editor: Peter Ache

Radboud University, Nijmegen, Netherlands

Routledge Research in Planning and Urban Design is a series of academic monographs for scholars working in these disciplines and the overlaps between them. Building on Routledge's history of academic rigour and cutting-edge research, the series contributes to the rapidly expanding literature in all areas of planning and urban design.

For a full list of titles in this series, please visit https://www.routledge.com/Routledge-Research-in-Planning-and-Urban-Design/book-series/RRPUD

# (Re)Generating Inclusive Cities

Poverty and Planning in
Urban North America

**Dan Zuberi and Ariel Taylor**

Routledge
Taylor & Francis Group

NEW YORK AND LONDON

First published 2018
by Routledge
52 Vanderbilt Avenue, New York, NY 10017

and by Routledge
2 Park Square, Milton Park, Abingdon, Oxon, OX14 4RN

First issued in paperback 2020

*Routledge is an imprint of the Taylor & Francis Group, an informa business*

© 2018 Taylor & Francis

*Library of Congress Cataloging-in-Publication Data*
A catalog record for this book has been requested

ISBN 13: 978-0-367-67048-1 (pbk)
ISBN 13: 978-1-138-20687-8 (hbk)

Typeset in Times New Roman
by Apex CoVantage, LLC

I would like to dedicate this book to the memory of my father-in-law, Campbell W. Robinson, a brilliant chemical engineering professor, progressive intellect, and much missed friend and grandfather.

—Dan Zuberi

I would like to dedicate this book to my mother, Lynn Taylor, for instilling in me a social and political consciousness that is forever with me.

—Ariel Taylor

# Contents

# Acknowledgments

I would like to thank the Social Sciences and Research Council of Canada (SSHRC), Canadian Institutes of Health Research (CIHR) New Investigator Salary Award, the Canadian Foundation for Innovation (CFI) Leaders Opportunity Fund (LOF), University of Toronto Connaught Fund grant, and a Royal Bank of Canada Chair for funding that contributed to this book. I also thank the University of Toronto Dean of the Factor-Inwentash Faculty of Social Work, Faye Mishna, and Director of the School of Public Policy and Governance, Peter Loewen, for their support. I also appreciate the support of my colleagues at the University of Toronto, including David Huchanski, Carmen Logie, Ito Peng, Arjumand Siddiqi, Philip Oreopoulos, Micheal Shier and Wes Shera. I also owe a debt of gratitude to my research assistants: Melita Ptashnick, Jade Nixon, Shani Kipang and Weijia Tan.

It has been a pleasure to collaborate with my co-author Ariel Taylor on this book and several other projects. Chapter 4 appeared originally in Michael Leary and John McCarthy, eds. *Urban Regeneration: A Handbook* (pp. 292–302). This chapter is reproduced with the permission of Routledge from Dan Zuberi and Ariel Taylor. *Urban Regeneration in Vancouver, Canada,* © Routledge, 2013. We have enjoyed working with the team at Routledge on this book, including Kathryn Schell, Nicole Solano and Krystal LaDuc. We also thank Denise A. File from Apex CoVantage for her production support.

I thank the following scholars for their support and mentorship over my career: Patricia Fernandez-Kelly, Neil Guppy, Christopher Jencks, Michèle Lamont, Peter A. Hall, Charles Hirschman, Katherine S. Newman, Jeffrey Reitz, George Smith, Mary C. Waters and William Julius Wilson. I also thank my colleagues: Irene Bloemraad, Sarah Brayne, Victor Chen, James R. Dunn, Anna Haley-Lock, Michael Halpin, Charles Hirschmann, David Tindall and Danielle van Jaarsveld.

I would like to thank some good friends: Joel Kamnitzer and Hannah Wachs, David Goldstein and Mindy Stricke, Sam Jones and Pierre Koch, Alan Jacobs and Antje Ellermann, Catherine Bischoff and Tom Zehetmeier,

Anand and Shilpa Das, Shannon Daub and Ryan Blogg, Veronique Sardi and John Parinello, Jeremy Weinstein and Rachel Gibson, Tamara Smyth and Tommy Babbin, Len and Denita Kagen, Jeremy Ledbetter and Eliana Cuevas, Wendy Roth and Ian Tietjen, Joiwind and Amit Ronen, David and Sarah Pinto-Duschinsky, Molly and Ty Sterkel and Trish Winston.

I would also like to thank my family: Anita Zuberi, Steve Chase and Annika Chuberi, Sofia, Jakob and Torsten Thorell, Michelle Robinson, Charles LePoutre, and Georges and Elise Robinson-LePoutre, Leslie Robinson, Graham Hildebrand and Kate Robinson, and Toni and David Owen. I especially appreciate the support of my mom, Lilly Zuberi. I owe my biggest debt of gratitude to my spouse, Joanna Robinson, and my daughters, Saskia and Naomi Robinson-Zuberi, for everything.

—Dan Zuberi

I would like to thank my co-author Dan Zuberi for many years of mentorship and collaboration, both on this and other projects. To Michelle Bonner, Marlea Clarke, Claire Cutler and Matt Murphy, thank you for your ongoing professional guidance and support. I am especially indebted to my family: Peter and Lynn Taylor, Judith Stapleton, Emma Taylor, Mike Bobbitt, and Walker and Callum Bobbitt. And lastly, to my partner, A. J. Shieck, who is limitless in his love and support for me in all things.

—Ariel Taylor

# Introduction

## Urban Renewal in North America in a Neoliberal Context

Cities today are essential economic, cultural and social hubs of global connectivity. As changing political and economic priorities push individuals out of suburban neighborhoods and into urban cores, planners and policymakers have embraced a variety of strategies to revitalize urban communities. In short, the twin processes of neoliberalism and urban renewal have worked to push and pull people into growing cities across North America. This book explores the social-spatial consequences of changing urban landscapes through policies of neoliberal urban regeneration. We pay particular attention to the confluence of urban mega-project development, strategies of residential social mixing, and brownfield cleanup. We contribute to a growing tradition of critical scholarship that seeks to better understand processes of "actually existing neoliberalism"[1] by focusing on the socio-spatial dislocation of the urban poor on both sides of the Canadian–American border. Despite historical differences in socioeconomic policy, we find that both countries face mounting socioeconomic pressure associated with urbanization. Gentrification, or the physical displacement of low-income by higher-income populations, is generated through the competitiveness of urban planning under conditions of neoliberal restructuring. However, despite the similarity of outcomes, processes of actually existing gentrification are far from homogenous and in turn open new possibilities for change. We argue the realization of more equitable and livable urban spaces can only be achieved through the inclusive regeneration of democratic urban communities.

Urban regeneration is widely understood as a process of socio-spatial change, driven by increased political and economic investment in urban landscapes and supported by heightened rates of urbanization. Once a prominent feature of the North American postwar Fordist economy, processes of urban regeneration have now been transformed under conditions of neoliberal restructuring. Neoliberalism constitutes both an idea and a set of processes (Jessop 2002; Hackworth 2007; Bridge et al. 2012). Conceptually, neoliberalism is the ideological rejection of egalitarian liberalism as practiced under the Keynesian welfare state. Defined by principles of individualism and laissez-faire economic decision making, neoliberalism embraces principles of market competition and applies them to social life. A rich body of literature spanning the social science disciplines now exists on neoliberalism as a political idea and epistemic phenomenon. However, less well documented are the myriad of often contradictory ways neoliberalism occurs in practice, in communities profoundly shaped by its political, economic and sociological implications. Recent works by Hackworth (2007), Leitner et al. (2007), Purcell (2008), Bridge et al. (2012) and others have attempted to demystify processes of neoliberal urban restructuring and the myriad ways in which urban landscapes are being transformed.

This introductory chapter begins with an historical overview of the rise of neoliberal economic policymaking and the ideological project it embodies. We chronicle four theoretical attempts to both make sense of neoliberal urban restructuring, while providing conceptual clarity. We introduce the concept of gentrification and link it to issues of social equity and justice, which are today central to critical perspectives on neoliberalism. We work

*Figure 0.1* Houseboats at Vancouver's Granville Island are dwarfed by new residential towers along False Creek

Photo by Dan Zuberi

to draw attention to the social-spatial displacement of the working class in cities on both sides of the Canadian–American border. Despite historical differences in social policy, both countries now face mounting pressure associated with rapid rates of urbanization and inequality.

## Economic Transformation and the Changing North American City

The North American postwar economy has profoundly shaped the contemporary landscape of urban communities. As the center of Fordist industrial mass production, cities like Detroit, Toronto and New York provided much of the capital needed to support both the welfare state and the often idyllic lifestyles associated with early twentieth-century suburbanization. However, in the postwar period, the growing need to attract new sources of capital led to the regeneration of urban spaces through large-scale infrastructure developments including expressways and office towers. Iconic projects such as Quincy Renaissance Center in Detroit, the CN Tower in Toronto and Place Villie Marie in Montreal transformed city skylines and put a generation of North Americans back to work. *Man-Made America* (Tunnard 1963) became the new doctrine of urban planning. Residential construction also flourished. Toronto's St. James Town and the Bronx's Co-Op City were residential projects at the time unprecedented in both cost and scale. The postwar metropolis was in short transformed through the application of modernist design principles and the proliferation of sprawl, producing a cityscape once sarcastically described by Jane Jacobs as "the radiant garden city beautiful" (1961, 25).

Beyond lacking a centralized planning vision or aesthetic appeal, the postwar urban metropolis was also criticized for displacing tens of thousands of North American families and contributing to the regressive distribution of socioeconomic benefits. Between 1949 and 1965, 1 million low-income residents were evicted from American cities in the name of both containing and eradicating blight (Weber 2002, 528). Inspired by a War on Poverty and supported by the Office of Economic Opportunity, the Community Action Program, and the Model Cities initiative, low-income urban communities were cast as sociologically and culturally deficient, rather than the victims of ongoing racial discrimination and labor market restructuring (Self & Sugrue 2002, 24). At the same time, suburbanization kept pace with the realization of high-end integrated communities such as New York's Long Island and Toronto's Don Mills, where shopping malls and recreation facilities provided both employment and leisure opportunities for those who could afford to participate. By the 1970s, more people lived in suburban communities than anywhere else in North America (Fowler 1995, 7). As capital investments shifted away from city centers and the manufacturing

*Figure 0.2* St. James Town is the largest high-rise community in Canada. Approximately 17,000 people live in its 19 towers and four low-rise apartment complexes.

Photo by Dan Zuberi

activities they housed, cities across North American entered the second half of the twentieth century fraught with not only economic pressures, but also shifting socio-political strategies to address them.

The neoliberal era of urban regeneration, beginning the 1980s and continuing through the present day, has been facilitated by the confluence of technological integration of a global marketplace and the increasingly service and consumer-based economy of Western countries. The speed of this restructuring has been facilitated by the depoliticization of market forces and the formation of new public–private partnership models of governance that critics argue work to conflate public with private interests. For example, the 'successful' regeneration of urban cores is now measured almost exclusively in terms of rising property values with little attention given to sociological indicators (Krumholz 1999, 84–85). From a global perspective, scholars now understand cities as nodes of transnational activity, facilitating the flow of economic, social and cultural processes in the form of labor, resources and capital (Castells 1996; Sassen 2001).

*Figure 0.3* Time Square, NYC is an iconic symbol of the contemporary urban landscape.

Photo by Dan Zuberi

However, at the level of the state, neoliberalism has not so much reduced the scope of government intervention, but rather transformed the nature of legal, political and economic decision making to both facilitate and encourage the growth of private sector activity. On the one hand, global economic restructuring and decreasing barriers to trade have profoundly limited the capacity of states to pursue independent or radically distinctive policymaking. One the other hand, neoliberalism has further decentralized political authority, empowering municipal city councilors and planning professionals to pursue significant reforms (Jessop 2002, 459–460). However, as cities move to foster 'smart growth' and market 'livable' urban communities, policymakers are less willing or able to provide the conditions necessary for citizen equality. Growing levels of socioeconomic inequality within North American cities in turn raises questions about both the quality and scope of citizen publics in the context of democratic political decision making.

While issues of social and economic equality have long troubled the tradition of liberal democracy, in North America, the Keynesian welfare state worked to guarantee a minimum level of security for its citizens. The erosion of public sector spending under conditions of neoliberalism have instead resulted in heightened levels of socioeconomic inequality and in turn a deficit in democratic participation (Purcell 2009, 144). The so-called renaissance of twenty-first-century urban landscapes is today contingent upon the dislocation of low-income individuals whose 'anti-social behavior' impedes highly profitable land valuation (Porter & Shaw 2009, 39–40). The criminalization of so-called anti-social behavior such as panhandling or squeegeeing through tough-on-crime policies in cities including NYC and Toronto works to hierarchically sort citizens based on their socioeconomic and cultural value. As processes of gentrification increasing result in the socio-spatial segregation of citizens into core and peripheral urban areas, critical scholars have increasingly brought their attention to bear on the problems and possibilities of the neoliberal city.

The following section outlines four critical perspectives on urban life under conditions of neoliberalism. The Entrepreneurial or Competitive City, the Creative City, the Revanchist City and, finally, the Just City will each be explored in turn. While not always mutually exclusive, these scholars point to the often-contradictory ways in which inequality is constituted in contemporary urban life. Marcuse and van Kempen (2000) have deemed the inner city a 'soft spot' for the implementation of neoliberal ideals, but it is here that alternative visions for urban life are also emerging. As such, we attempt to answer calls for alternative forms of regeneration, forms that perhaps offer possibilities for more equitable, sustainable and just urban futures.

*Figure 0.4* Residents of Boston gather to take in a street performance in a downtown park.

Photo by Dan Zuberi

## Four 'Cities'

Nearly two decades ago, David Harvey (1989) described a shift "from managerialism to entrepreneurialism" in strategies of urban governance. Unlike the redistributive and labor-focused approach typical of urban governance in the 1960s, Harvey argued a new political consensus had emerged, beginning in the late 1970s, that cities should adopt more entrepreneurial approaches to economic development. In other words, the focus of urban governance was no longer understood to include the provision of services to urban residents or the demands of organized labor, but instead required municipal authorities to attract and retain new sources of business and private investment. Competition, it was argued, was now a necessary part of policymaking. The Entrepreneurial City adopted the logic of market competition and applied it to urban life.

Municipal governments conceded to market forces by reducing taxes and reforming regulations, while at the same time reallocating public funding to education, infrastructure, and services supportive of business development. Public–private partnership (P3s) agreements quickly became an integral part of regenerated urban landscapes. As a market-based solution to the increasingly criticized federal urban renewal program in the United States, P3s were further encouraged through the introduction of the Urban Development Acton Grant program introduced in 1977.

The U.S. Urban Development Action Grant program required municipal governments to compete with one another for limited and largely piecemeal federal funding. Applicants were encouraged to pursue private partnership agreements to leverage more private sector resources to augment federal support (Jonas & McCarthy 2010, 39). However, critics pointed to the speculative nature of P3 projects that also required cities to assume significant financial risk. As municipal governments took on increasing liability, many private sector companies benefitted tremendously through large influxes of public money (Harvey 1989, 7). Moreover, 'success' in urban development, which increasingly included P3 developments, did not necessarily translate into lower poverty or unemployment rates. Krumholz (1999, 85) notes that in 1980, 16.5 percent of U.S. urban residents lived in poverty, while a decade later the figure was 18.7 percent. The idea that municipal councilors should first and foremost use their resources, not to fight poverty, but to placate corporate and financial interests that, in the context of inter-city competition, may choose to relocate to more business-friendly locales has today become widely accepted (Hackworth 2007, 2).

The Entrepreneurial or Competitive City is predicated on market competition, fiscal conservatism, privatization and deregulation of planning (Kipfer & Keil 2002, 236). These governance strategies are employed to proactively foster an investment climate amenable to the expansion of private enterprise; enterprises that could and ostensibly will relocate if operational constraints are imposed. Consequently, cities must engage in competitive strategies of accumulation, the results of which are deemed to be part and parcel of public interest. Conversely, regulations that safeguard collective bargaining rights, enhance environmental protections or promote safe and equitable working environments are understood to distort the efficiency of markets and in turn the individual maximization of profit (Purcell 2008, 16). Yet as shifting economic strategies also work to transform markets for urban real estate, employment opportunities and the provision of social security, the constitution of urban publics are also changing. As a new generation of educated, professional and creative young adults descend on urban cores in cities across North America, low-income, low-skilled and ostensibly unproductive populations are being increasingly displaced.

While the Entrepreneurial or Competitive City works to attract new source of capital into urban communities, the Creative City is designed for a new population of urban workers. Popularized by the work of Richard Florida (2002; 2005), the urban 'creative class' is dominated by highly skilled, technologically advanced and well-paid young professionals who are attracted to urban cores for the services and livability they provide. Policymakers in cities across North America have, often inspired by Florida's ideas, moved to provide the kind of aesthetic and branding sought by this elite group of creative workers, while at the same time rolling back protections that once aided traditionally blue-collar urban industries such as manufacturing. The fostering of a 24-hour downtown, the proliferation of entertainment and luxury shopping districts and live-work rental spaces all work to promote creative cities. While diversity remains a cornerstone of creative city planning, critics argue the resulting policies of residential social mix pathologize poverty, while doing little to ensure equity among urban populations (Lees 2008; Peck 2005; Ley 2003; Musterd & Ostendorf 2000).

While the creative class ethic of urban professionals values social diversity, it does not necessarily value equity (Fainstein 2005). Diversity in this sense is promoted as a strategy to attract human capital, facilitate innovation and support progressivism, particularly in the context of gay and lesbian communities. For the Competitive City, diversity acts to stimulate economic investment in goods and services that support creative growth. Yet the import of the creative class can go hand in hand with gentrification, which works to out-price lower-income individuals from urban core. The diversity that remains can be limited to groups able to keep up with rising costs of living. Even Florida recognizes that

> While the creative class favors openness and diversity, to some degree it is a diversity of elites, limited to highly educated creative people. Even though the rise of the Creative Class has opened up new avenues of advancement for women and members of ethnic minorities, its existence has certainly failed to put an end to long-standing divisions of race and gender. Within high-tech industries in particular these divisions still seem to hold.
>
> (Florida 2002, 80)

In this sense, sociological and economic exclusions remain firmly intertwined. As Fainstein (2005, 14) notes, by fostering creative urban communities, we have largely lost sight of the importance of generating employment and living situations for those excluded from creative enterprises. In short, not everyone can be creative. Instead, the pathologization and even criminalization of the urban poverty that remains has worked to discipline so-called anti-social behavior and further regulate the use the public space. The pursuit of basic human survival needs—such as a dry place to sleep, a bath-room, or the procurement of spare change to purchase food—are increasingly limited as cities compete for heightened standards of 'livability', all the while denying a basic standard of living to its most vulnerable residents.

While the integration of culture and aesthetic diversity into urban design has enhanced the competitiveness of many North American cities, it has simultaneously imposed set of class-based sensibilities that work to limit how urban space is and can be utilized. A growing body of critical scholarship now shows how the regulation and securitization of public space is achieved through the criminalization of anti-social or unwelcome behavior (Madanipour 2010; O'Grady et al. 2013; Chesnay et al. 2013; Kohn 2013). Policymakers have increasingly sought to curb oftentimes already declining crime rates by cracking down on signs of disorder such as graffiti, panhandling, squeegeeing and vandalism. Moreover, the privatization of public spaces, including parks and promenades, have also worked to regulate life in urban cores, transforming spaces once associated with the formation of social capital and civic engagement into liabilities and untapped sources of profit in an evolving marketplace (Madanipour 2010).

*Figure 0.5* Graffiti on display in San Francisco's Mission district
Photo by Dan Zuberi

The influential work of William Julius Wilson (1987, 1996) warned that high-poverty neighborhoods would eventually suffer from disintegration and ghetto-related behaviors including criminality, gang violence and dysfunctional family structures. This depiction of low-income urban areas mirrored that of James Wilson and George Kelling (1982), whose broken windows theory promoted zero-tolerance policies for combatting crime. Wilson and Kelling perceived low-income neighborhoods as breeding grounds for more serious crime. The perceived benefits of functionally and socially mixed urban communities, including support for diversity, have driven the mass-scale redevelopment of urban housing across North America.

While support for residential social mix first emerged in the 1960s in response to the homogenization and social-spatial segregation of urban/suburban populations, by the 1990s, its foundations and ideological justification had been fundamentally transformed under neoliberalism. The mixed-income communities advocated by scholars and advocates such as Jane Jacobs in the 1960s were thought to promote civic engagement through the fostering of trust and the generation of social capital. Conversely, today social mixing is seen largely as the *solution* to disruptive or 'anti-social' public behavior. Securing the city for the mounting number of upper-middle class residents through strategies like social mixing and the regulation of public behavior remains an important component of neoliberal governance (Lees 2008; Bridge et al. 2012; Hackworth 2007).

Indeed, a growing shortage of affordable urban housing and the heightened regulation of downtown public spaces are just some of the growing pains associated with the evolution of the neoliberal city—pains that are experienced in profoundly social and spatialized patterns of exclusion. Disputes over the allocation and use of increasingly high-density urban spaces are rooted in conflicting claims to ownership and the use of space. Smith (1996) employed the term 'revanchist' to describe what he sees as a discourse of revenge against the urban poor who, in historically monopolizing urban spaces, are in turn deemed responsible for its decay. In this context, marginal communities are targeted as sites of insecurity that require legal action in order to "sanitize public spaces" (Chesnay et al. 2013, 162).

In contrast to the Entrepreneurial and Creative City concepts, the Revanchist City captures a set of administrative policies—policing, social housing, the management of public space, that work to redefine the social orientation of urban publics. The moral undertones of governance strategies that privilege consumers over citizens is, according to Kipfer and Keil, made visible through coercive forms of social control (2002, 237). From the perspective of low-income and impoverished urban communities, the imposition of a new creative and competitive urban landscape is "an undemocratic imposition of a particularist vision masquerading as the public interest" (Fainstein 2005, 7).

Neoliberalism, for many scholars, raises important concerns about the democratic capacity of many low-income people to overcome the ascendant power of capital in the governance of public life (Hardt & Negri 2004; Dryzek 1996; Bowles & Gintis 1986). According to Purcell,

> To the extent that neoliberalization succeeds in its agenda to augment the power of corporations vis-à-vis the state (Hardt & Negri 2004), and insofar as liberal-democratic states are the principle representative of the mass of people, neoliberalization produces a democratic deficit because it transfers power from democratic citizens to corporations.
>
> (Purcell 2008, 24)

In an effort to recapture the democratic 'right to the city' (Lefebvre 1968; Purcell 2002), scholars have begun to articulate a Just City alternative (Fainstein 2010; Harvey 2012).

Arguable, the city is both large enough for democratic governments to enjoy considerable influence, yet at the same time small enough for the realization of a democratic culture that allows for people to affect political decision making (Connolly & Steil 2009). However, according to Fainstein,

> Developing an appropriate physical setting for a heterogeneous urbanity, however, can go only so far in the generation of a just city. Most crucial is a political consciousness that supports progressive moves at national and local levels toward respectfulness of others and greater equality.
>
> (Fainstein 2005, 16)

Significantly, Fainstein and others adopt a normative position on justice that favors social equity over and above individualization. While this remains an important source of tension within liberal-democratic debate, issues of equity are central to relational understandings of the interdependence of individuals and communities (Campbell 2006, 101) and calls for more inclusive political participation. While resistance to socio-spatial segregation in across North American urban centers is growing, alternative approaches remain largely disparate and uneven in their successes. To achieve the goal of fostering the expansion of Just City communities, much more needs to be done to build coherence across localities. It is in this spirit that we hope to move toward a new understanding of how to build more inclusive, equitable and socially just urban communities.

## (Re)Generating Inclusive Cities

While the ideas that support neoliberalism continue to sustain changing approaches to urban governance, processes of neoliberalism require acute sensitivity to the great variety of urban regeneration experiences. The restructuring of national and urban economies toward recreation and consumption activities reserved for the enjoyment of affluent individuals alone has not been all encompassing or without alternative strategies of resistance. While urban regeneration has more often than not opened the door to gentrification, we largely agree with Porter and Shaw (2009) that the two are not synonymous, nor is the later an inevitable result of the former.

The following chapters explore the confluence of three avenues of urban regeneration, typically understood as part and parcel of neoliberalization: mega-projects, residential social mix and brownfield cleanup. Mega-project development has been facilitated since the 1970s by an upswing in P3 project financing and attempts by cities to gain a competitive edge in development of new business opportunities. In Chapter 1, we explore trends in mega-project development in several North American cities in an effort to highlight similarities and differences in issues of urban equity. We ask: What is the role of mega-project development in reinforcing growing social-spatial polarization in urban cores? How do mega-projects impact quality of life among urban populations, and what alternative models currently exist governing their operation? An in-depth analysis of mega-project development in Boston, New York City and Montreal help to excavate how issues of access and privilege are bound up in the neoliberalization of large-scale public infrastructure projects.

Chapter 2 brings the focus to urban neighborhoods and initiatives to revitalize residential communities. We first explore broader urban policies aimed at promoting residential social mix and examine how they have shaped contemporary regeneration projects in several North American cities. Despite efforts to move away from the postwar model of demolition and relocation of urban 'ghettos', decentralization of low-income populations has, perhaps unwittingly, reinforced the stigmatization of urban poverty. The shift toward mixed-income and high-density urban communities is explored through the HOPE VI program in the United States, as well as the redevelopment of Canada's largest social housing project, Toronto's Regent Park. We end the chapter with an exploration of an alternative model of residential urban development, undertaken in Seattle, which takes seriously issues of social equity by engaging in a participatory planning process.

In Chapter 3, we explore the emerging trend of brownfield cleanup and development. Perhaps the most disparate and un-regularized component of neoliberal regeneration, brownfields offer a compelling frontier of urban development, but are increasingly subject to forces of gentrification. Without coherent and community-centered management strategies brownfields risk contributing to the social-spatial dislocation of urban communities who have long been unequally burdened by the heightened environmental contamination of brownfield land. A central tenet of urban environmental sustainability and aesthetic revitalization, brownfield cleanup and development raises important questions about the right to occupy safe, clean and welcoming urban spaces. We explore a number of ways in which governments and communities are exerting control over brownfield development in the face of increasing pressure to free up value urban real estate for market valuation. In many former industrial urban cores, such as those found in Detroit, Toronto and Brooklyn, brownfields represent the last parcels of urban land available for substantive redevelopment. Brownfields thus occupy a powerful space of potential transformation.

Chapter 4 works to bring together each of governance themes explored in previous chapters by examining their impact in a single urban locale. Vancouver, Canada, is a leading example of post-industrial urban design and livability where mega-project developments, such as those generated by the 2012 Winter Olympics, have occurred in tandem with residential social mixing and brownfield cleanup. This chapter provides an in-depth examination of how one city is impacted by neoliberal policymaking and the consequences these trends now pose for the city's poor.

Chapter 5 then takes a step back and evaluates contemporary trends in urban regeneration in North America. In the context of suburbanization, deindustrialization and neoliberalism, what do we see as the primary driving processes shaping the process and outcomes of initiatives today and in the near future in North America? Whereas the introductory chapter has provided a conceptual overview of problems of gentrification—including social-spatial dislocation, stigmatization and inequality—Chapter 5 draws on empirical evidence to illustrate where we in cities across North America currently stand. In clearly articulating the challenges, as they exist across urban spaces, we set the groundwork for policy recommendations made in the final chapter.

The final concluding chapter builds on a synthesis of much of the analysis presented in prior chapters to advance theoretical development in the areas of contemporary urban policy and planning. We attempt to situate North American cities in a more global context by considering the experiences of a number of European metropolises. North American cities are experiencing a new stage and unique stage of regeneration and development, heavily influenced by neoliberalism and tensions between economic growth, equity, promoting diversity, inclusion, and government investment and retrenchment. We reflect on the how these forces have changed urban development and renewal patterns, bringing us into the era of the condo-boom, an era of urban renaissance for some, but continued and perhaps even greater social exclusion for others. Finally, we present a number of creative and innovative policy recommendations to support improved urbanism and urban regeneration in the North American context. These recommendations include investments in accessible social housing, participatory planning initiatives and inclusive public spaces, with the goal of mitigating the dislocations caused by neoliberal urban regeneration and promoting the just, inclusive city as the North American city of the future. As urban planning strategies, along with their governance mechanisms, attempt to address many of the challenges associated with neoliberal economic restructuring, we pause to consider their sociological implications. While we recognize many of the pressures currently shaping life across North American cities, we take this opportunity to insist upon a vision of urban life that includes both equity and diversity along both social and spatial dimensions.

## References

Bowles, S., and Gintis, H. (1986) *Democracy and Capitalism: Property, Community, and Contradictions of Modern Social Thought.* New York, NY: Basic Books.

Bridge, G., Butler, T., and Lees, L. (2012) *Mixed Communities: Gentrification by Stealth?* Bristol, UK: The Policy Press.

Campbell, H. (2006) "Just Planning: The Art of Situated Ethical Judgement", *Journal of Planning Education and Research*, 26: 92–106.

Castells, M. (1996) *The Rise of the Network Society.* Oxford, UK: Blackwell Publishers.

Chesnay, C., Bellot, C., and Sylvestre, M. (2013) "Taming Disorderly People One Ticket at a Time: The Penalization of Homelessness in Ontario and British Columbia", *The Canadian Journal of Criminology and Criminal Justice*, 55(2): 161–185.

Connolly, J., and Steil, J. (2009) "Introduction: Finding Justice in the City", In P. Marcuse, J. Connolly, J. Novy, I. Olivo, C. Potter, and J. Steil (eds.), *Searching for the Just City: Debates in Urban Theory and Practice.* New York, NY: Routledge. Pp. 1–16.

Dryzek. J. (1996) *Democracy in Capitalist Times: Ideals, Limits, and Struggles.* Oxford, UK: Oxford Universtiy Press.

Fainstein, S. (2005) "Cities and diversity: Should We Want It? Can We Plan for It?" *Urban Affairs Review*, 41(1): 3–19.

Fainstein, S. (2010) *The Just City.* Ithaca, NY: Cornell University Press.

Florida, R. (2002) *The Rise of the Creative Class: And How it's Transforming Working, Leisure, Community, and Everyday Life.* New York, NY: Basic Books.

Florida, R. (2005) *Cities and the Creative Class.* New York: Routledge.

Fowler, E.P. (1995) *Building Cities that Work.* Kingston, ON: McGill-Queen's University Press.

Hackworth, J. (2007) *The Neoliberal City: Governance, Ideology, and Development in American Urbansim.* Ithaca, NY: Cornell University Press.

Hardt, M., and Negri, A. (2004) *Multitude: War and Democracy in the Age of Empire*. New York, NY: Penguin.

Harvey, D. (2012) *Rebel City: From the Right to the City to the Urban Revolution*. New York, NY: Verso.

Harvey, D. (1989) "From Managerialism to Entrepreneurialism: The Transformation in Urban Governance in Late Capitalism", *Geographical Analysis*, 71B: 3–17.

Jacobs, J. (1961) *The Death and Life of Great American Cities*. New York, NY: Random House.

Jessop, B. (2002) "Liberalism, Neoliberalism, and Urban Governance: A State-Theoretical Perspective", *Antipode*, 34(3): 452–472.

Jonas, A.E., and McCarthy, L. (2010) "Redevelopment at All Costs? A Critical Review and Examination of the American Model of Urban Management and Regeneration", In J. Diamond, J. Liddle, A. Southern, and P. Osei (eds.), *Urban Regeneration Management: International Perspectives*. New York, NY: Routledge. Pp. 31–62.

Kipfer, S., and Keil, R. (2002) "Toronto inc? Planning the Competitive City in the New Toronto", *Antipode*, 34(2): 227–264.

Kohn, M. (2013) "Privatization and Protest: Occupy Wall Street, Occupy Toronto, and the Occupation of Public Space in a Democracy", *Perspectives on Politics*, 11: 99–110.

Krumholz, N. (1999) "Equitable Approaches to Local Economic Development", *Policy Studies Journal*, 27(1): 83–95.

Lees, L. (2008) "Gentrification and Social Mixing: Towards and Inclusive Urban Renaissance?" *Urban Studies*, 45(12): 2449–2470.

Lefebvre, H. (1968) *Le Droit à la ville*. Paris: Anthropos.

Leitner, H., Peck, J., and Sheppard, E.S. (2007) *Contesting Neoliberalism: Urban Frontiers*. New York, NY: Guildford Press.

Ley, D. (2003) "Artists, Aestheticisation and the Field of Gentrification", *Urban Studies*, 40: 2527–2544.

Madanipour, A. (2010) *Whose Public Space? International Cases in Urban Design and Development*. New York, NY: Routledge.

Marcuse, P., and van Kempen, R. (2000) "Conclusion: A Changed Spatial Order", In P. Marcuse and R. van Kempen (eds.), *Globalizing Cities: A New Spatial Order?* Oxford, UK: Blackwell Publishing.

Musterd, S., and Ostendorf, W. (2000) *Urban Segregation and the Welfare State: Inequality and Exclusion in Western Cities*. New York, NY: Routledge.

O'Grady, B., Gaetz, S., and Buccieri, K. (2013) "Tickets. . .and More Tickets: A Case Study of the Enforcement of the Ontario Safe Streets Act", *Canadian Public Policy*, 39(4): 541–558.

Peck, J. (2005) "Struggling with the creative class", *International Journal of Urban and Regional Research*, 29.4, 740–770.

Porter, L., and Shaw, K. (2009) *Whose Urban Renaissance? An International Comparison of Urban Regeneration Strategies*. New York, NY: Routledge.

Purcell, M. (2009) "Resisting Neoliberalization: Communicative Planning or Counter-Hegemonic Movements?" *Planning Theory*, 8(2): 140–165.

Purcell, M. (2008) *Recapturing Democracy: Neoliberalization and the Struggle for Alternative Urban Futures*. New York, NY: Routledge.

Purcell, M. (2002) "Excavating Lefebvre: The Right to the City and its Urban Politics of the Inhabitant", *GeoJournal*, 58: 99–108.

Sassen, S. (2001) *The Global City: New York, London, Tokyo*. Princeton, NJ: Princeton University Press.

Self, R.O., and Sugrue, J.T. (2002) "The Power of Place", In J.C. Agnew and R. Rosenwieg (eds.), *A Companion to Post-1945 America*. Malden, MA: Blackwell Publishing. Pp. 20–43.

Smith, N. (1996) *The New Urban Frontier: Gentrification and the Revanchist City*. New York, NY: Routledge.

Tunnard, C. (1963) *Man-Made America: Chaos or Control? An Inquiry into Selected Problems of Design in the Urbanized Landscape*. New Haven, CT: Yale University Press.

Weber, R. (2002) "Extracting Value from the City: Neoliberalism and Urban Redevelopment", *Antipode*, 34(3): 519–540

Wilson, W.J. (1996) *When Work Disappears: The World of the New Urban Poor*. Vintage Books: New York, NY.

Wilson, W.J. (1987) *The Truly Disadvantaged: The Inner City, the Underclass and Public Policy*. University of Chicago Press: Chicago, IL.

Wilson, W.J., and Kelling, G. (1982) "Broken Windows: The Police and Neighborhood Safety", *Atlantic Monthly*, 249(3): 29–38.

# 1 Mega-projects From the Big Dig to the High Line

## Regenerating the City

The history of mega-project development in North America is intimately bound up in processes of state-led industrialization and the postwar urban economy. Between the 1950s and late 1970s, mega-project development was capital-intensive, but also fiscally and ideologically sustained by a Keynesian welfare state. In this context, major infrastructure projects were conceptualized to provide not only improved critical public services (e.g., hospitals or freeways), but also socioeconomic benefits (including both housing and employment) that were considered part and parcel of a prevailing modernizing and democratic spirit (Lehrer & Laidley 2008, 788). However, many mega-projects of this era also boast legacies of massive price tags, severe environmental degradation, and flawed design. Criticized on both the left and the right, mega-projects of the North American postwar era were often either socially disruptive, regressive and displacing, or unwarranted governmental interventions in the market and the unjustifiable confiscation of private property (Orueta & Fainstein 2008, 759).

By the late 1970s and early 1980s, state-sponsored mega-projects were increasingly argued to be fiscally irresponsible. In the context of growing economic instability globally, public–private partnerships began to emerge as a market-based solution to contain unsustainable costs and other risks associated with mega-project development initiatives. In the United States, the federal Urban Development Action Grant program provided cities sizable funds to "help stimulate economic development activity needed to aid in economic recovery" (Young 1984, 112). The program required substantial private sector investment, promoted public consultation, and awarded funds on a discretionary basis, promoting competition between cities (see Young 1984). The entrepreneurialism associated with programs like the Urban Development Action Grant came to define what some scholars have called the neoliberalization of the post-federal era in American cities (Clarke & Gaile 1992; Brenner & Theodore 2002; Jonas & McCarthy 2010). This new urban landscape was guided by principles of free market competition, consumerism and creative entrepreneurialism as cities increasingly fought to attract both talent and capital in a global marketplace.

The global recession and political turmoil of the late 1980s led to the prioritization of national over regional economic planning and helped to produce a "chilly climate" in cities across North America (Clarke & Gaile 1992, 188). Forced to find alternative sources of funding, local officials increasingly turned to private investors and foreign direct investment for financing of mega-projects creating a more politicized, less transparent planning processes. States facilitated the legal, economic and political parameters necessary for mega-project development, while at the same time encouraging decentralized political control and strategies of market-led growth. In short, the mega-projects of late-twentieth-century North America "profoundly reworked the institutional infrastructure upon which Fordist-Keynesian capitalism was grounded" (Brenner & Theodore 2002, 349). At the same time, that cities experienced powerful fiscal constraints, public–private partnership models transformed the governance regimes of urban communities, limiting accountability and subsequently exacerbating tensions between public and private interests.

Public–private mega-project developments flourished in the late 1980s to include vast complexes of mixed-use designed to promote cities within an increasingly competitive global economy. These large-scale and concentrated mega-projects became "integrated into the international property and financial market and/or global socio-cultural networks" in order for cities to "actively reposition themselves within the global economy" (Lehrer & Laidley 2008, 798). However, mega-project developments have a well-documented history of social and economic exclusion, which has led some authors to argue that "displacement is intrinsic to mega-project development" (Gellert & Lynch 2003, 15).

Jonas and McCarthy argue that rather than managing the socioeconomic consequences of mega-project development, cities are increasingly promoting "growth first" or "growth at all costs" rather than fulfilling their democratic obligations to citizens (2010, 33–34). Moreover, flexible labor markets, the rise in precarious working conditions and low-paid jobs work to exacerbate problems of affordable urban housing (Kadi & Musterd 2014, 249), a phenomenon scholars note is no longer isolated to the United States. Even traditionally social democratic cities of Western Europe and Canada now struggle to balance rising real estate and luxury markets with historical commitments to equity and social security (Orueta & Fainstein 2008; Fainstein 2008).

Critics of public–private mega-project developments argue that limited accountability and a lack of public participation produce negative impacts and costly correctives. In other words, by conflating private with public interests, neoliberal planning processes work to support the interests of private capital above and beyond those of public citizens. According to Bornstein:

> [W]hile benefits from such projects are likely to accrue at a municipal or regional level, residents in nearby areas incur many disamenities, whether through displacement or to accommodate the facilities, increased traffic, noise and air pollution, or a shift to non-residential uses in the area. For all these reasons, the literature identifies mega-projects as a factor increasing spatial and socio-economic polarization in contemporary cities.
>
> (Bornstein 2007, 3)

Since the 1980s, mega-project planners and promoters have responded to community critiques of 'old' mega-projects by designing more inclusive planning processes, and taking measures to mitigate the most damaging social and environmental impacts of earlier schemes.

Proposed new freeway or transit projects that bisect existing urban communities or sensitive ecological habitats are now often built underground to minimize disruption on the surface, a process Altshuler and Luberoff (2003) term "do no harm planning". Massive land redevelopment schemes also commonly eschew the concentration of single land uses in favor of a combination of public housing, private market housing, institutions and parks, facilities that appeal to a wide range of constituencies. New city building strategies, such as community development partnerships and community benefiting agreements, have been employed in an attempt to have mega-projects better meet the concerns of local residents and low-income households (Altshuler & Luberoff 2003; Fainstein 2008; Lehrer & Laidley 2008; Siemiatycki 2013, 172–173).

Given these developments, we interrogate and explore the 'actually existing' consequences of mega-project development in the context of neoliberal urban planning. We first draw on the experiences of two iconic mega-projects located in the Northeastern United State that taken together epitomize the ideological and functional implications of the new urban economy. In Boston, MA, the Central Artery Tunnel project—popularly referred to as the Big Dig—transformed the city's downtown core over its 15 years of construction at a cost of $14.6 billion. In New York City, the opening of the High Line pedestrian promenade has repositioned the city, and its West Chelsea neighborhood, as a global leader in sustainable restoration and design. However, despite both projects' relative success, we ask how low-income and other marginalized communities have been uniquely impacted? We argue that both projects reveal important social-spatial consequences associated with the neoliberal city, but also maintain that important alternatives do exist. We examine efforts to accommodate broader community consultation and participation in mega-project developments on both sides of the U.S.–Canada border, in San Francisco, CA, and Montreal, Québec. These cases provide potentially important counter-examples to the dominant trend of sweeping neoliberal regeneration, particularly in areas where low-income communities reside.

## Boston, MA: The Big Dig

Boston's Central Artery Tunnel Project, or 'Big Dig', was conceived and promoted as the solution to significant traffic congestion along the city's interstate running through the downtown core. Chronic congestion along the elevated six-lane highway had long been problematic. While in 1959 approximately 75,000 vehicles per day traversed this 1.5-mile stretch of road, by 1990, more than 190,000 vehicles a day utilized this route. City planners projected escalating traffic jams and commuters routinely complained of long waits and poor air quality (Fein 2012, 48). Moreover, the 40-foot-high walls supporting the congested expressway effectively cut off the city from the waterfront, an area where homelessness and blight had long been present (Robinson 2008). In short, both policymakers, along with the city's business community, promoted a mega-project development solution including a new artery route and tunnel under Boston Harbor. Official planning began in 1982 and construction in 1991. However, increasingly burdened by a number of timely and expensive setbacks, the project would not be completed until 2007.

Substantively Boston's Big Dig included a number of infrastructure projects and roadway redevelopments. In addition to rerouting the elevated central artery (Interstate 93) into a new 3.5-mile (5.6 km) tunnel, plans for a second tunnel connecting Instate 90 to Logan International Airport, as well as a new bridge crossing the Charles River, were also pursued. Finally, the newly accessible waterfront space, created by leveling the elevated expressway and rerouting traffic underground, was to become flagship green-space allocated for public use. However, to qualify for federal financial assistance, the project quickly ballooned in scope resulting in heightened bureaucracy, unanticipated costs and growing opposition (Fein 2012; Bearfield & Dubnick 2007; Bushouse 2002). Now complete, we examine the Big Dig's legacy for those residents of Boston most directly impacted by this mega-project development, particularly those now adjacent to the downtown core. By emphasizing the New Urbanist design principles and the social-spatial reorganization created by the Big Dig, we highlight how actually existing neoliberal regeneration can, despite notable efforts at consultation and mitigation, rapidly gentrify low-income areas, producing substantial challenges for pre-existing urban communities.

Beginning in the early 1980s, Boston enjoyed substantial economic prosperity, with the number of wage and salary jobs increasing by nearly 10 percent. However, Boston was and remains a commuter city and, as such, upwards of 60 percent of jobs during this period were filled by non-city residents (those residing in the suburbs who worked, but did not live, downtown) (Hellman et al. 1997, 116). In short, the economic benefits of growth to Boston residents during this period should not be overstated, but it does help to explain the economic and political will behind Boston's highway regeneration. However, while annual wages rose sharply over the decade, by 1989, the state of Massachusetts entered a severe economic recession. Between 1988 and 1992, the total number of wage and salary jobs in Boston declined by 12 percent, most notably from the city's construction and manufacturing industries (Hellman et al. 1997, 117). Significantly, it was within the context of economic stagnation that in 1984, proponents of Boston's Central Artery/Tunnel Project—otherwise known as the Big Dig—sought federal assistance for project financing.

To meet the requirements for federal assistance, the Big Dig was significantly expanded to increase both the main tunnel's capacity and coverage. After initially being vetoed by President Reagan in 1987, Congress later approved funding for the project and ground was broken in 1991. With an initial price tag of $2.8 billion USD, subsequent projections estimated costs associated with the Big Dig to run upwards of $14 billion USD (Bushouse 2002, 54). While in the 1980s, the Boston's unemployment rate was just under 5 percent, by 1991, it had risen to 8.6 percent despite significant population decline (Hellman et al. 1997, 117). According to some, the Big Dig, and the associated cleanup of the Boston Harbor, contributed to reversing this trend (Hellman et al. 1997 1997, 118). However, in 1997 responsibility for and oversight of the project were transferred from the Massachusetts Highway Department and Governor's Office to the Massachusetts Turnpike Authority (MTA), who in turn partnered in a joint venture. The project's privatization in turn led to a steep decline in wages and salaried employment in Boston during the same period, in addition to significantly reducing independent oversight and public accountability (Bearfield & Dubnick 2007).

By transferring ownership to the Massachusetts Turnpike Authority, the project became effectively insolated from government oversight, which in turn contributed to ballooning costs and construction shortcuts. Fein (2012) documents how conflicts over the provision of financial responsibility, project management and accountability plagued the project's development and contributed to its mounting price tag. A major leak in 2004 caused a backup in traffic spanning nearly 10 miles and raised important questions about the project's safety. Two years later, 12 tons of concrete collapsed from the tunnel's ceiling killing one motorist and injuring countless others. Fein concludes, "the structure of public–private collaboration and consequent limitations on oversight appeared to be at the root of the Big Dig's predicament" (Fein 2012, 160).

Jennings (2004) too argues that the privatization process had spill over affects in downtown communities impacted by the Big Dig. Despite affecting predominantly non-white neighborhoods, there was "relatively little participation on the part of people of color in terms of holding business contracts of significant size or jobs in the labor pool" as well as providing "relatively few decentralized capital investments for neighborhoods" (Jennings 2004, 19). All this raises questions about the legacy of the Big Dig for communities in Boston, particularly those areas subject to processes of gentrification. As newly accessible waterfront and increasingly manicured green spaces replaced the formerly elevated expressway, lower-income populations suddenly faced new pressures of dislocation.

By relocating an elevated roadway underground, the Big Dig served to open up prime urban real estate to both public and private use. Subsequent land-use projects such as the Rose F. Kennedy Greenway—a 15-acre green throughway linking several downtown neighborhoods and consisting of landscaped gardens, public fountains and art projects— transformed long-established and predominately immigrant communities such as Boston's North End and Roxbury neighborhoods. Celebrated as an achievement in heightened accessibility and green urban design, steeply rising housing costs and accompanying shifts in demographic trends in residency suggest not all Bostonians have benefited or benefited equally. Couched in the language of New Urbanism and Smart Growth, the Big Dig exemplifies some of the shortcomings of planning models that "overlook the critical role of political power in terms of who has it and how it is used to maintain social and economic benefits for certain interests" (Jennings 2004, 14). Reflective of the pro-growth, neoliberal logic of urban development the Big Dig may have succeeded in generating new businesses and expanding market opportunities for some, but this has been achieved in part at the expense of low-income individuals and urban communities.

Boston is home to a diverse population with approximately 45 percent of residents identifying as ethnic or racial minorities. However, the city's neighborhoods also continue to remain relatively segregated by race and ethnicity (Robinson 2008, 48). With 33 universities and colleges located within Boston's city limits, and approximately 60 located within the Boston metropolitan area, the city continues to struggle with the challenge of

*Figure 1.1* A food vendor parked along the Rose F. Kennedy Greenway, Boston
Photo by Dan Zuberi

underemployed or unemployed young adults and families. These populations face a relatively high cost of living compared to elsewhere in the United States, a trend that urban regeneration contributes to. In 2000, for example, the average one-bedroom rental unit in downtown Boston was priced just under $1,000 USD/month.[1] By 2015, the University of Massachusetts ranked Boston the third most expensive rental market in the country with median one-bedroom rental units costing approximately $2,280 per month.[2]

While considerable amounts of funding were allocated to mitigation efforts during both the initial and later expansionist stages of the Big Dig development, its impacts have nonetheless been considerable. Having avoided a return to the urban renewal policies of the 1950s where low-income housing developments were simply demolished in order to attract suburban—predominantly white—families back downtown, Governor Michael Dukakis's promise not to take a single-family home turned out to be more hyperbole than reality (see Bushouse 2002). Just as Tajima (2003) prophetically warned:

> When a property price increases as a result of environmental improvement, property owners enjoy the windfalls through the capitalization effects. On the other hand, tenants may be required to pay more rent to keep up with the housing market as urban amenities attract high-income population groups. In that case, low-income minorities who rent apartments in the inner city could be worse off. As their rent rise, they may not be able to continue to live in their current residence.
>
> (Tajima 2003, 652)

While Dukakis kept his promise to keep the bulldozers at bay, displacement by market forces and rental price increases has most certainly hurt the urban poor. In 2004, the *Boston Globe* reported that commercial properties along the old Artery had increased in value by nearly 80 percent, a rate of change nearly double the citywide average (Gelinas 2007). Proponents of the Big Dig point to the benefits of growth for spurring economic investment and boosting tax revenues in addition to job creation and heightened disposable incomes. However as residents of Boston's poorest community of Roxbury have found, reconciling local priorities for growth and development can be in tension with an agenda that aims to make businesses more competitive and populations more entrepreneurial, and can push the marginal into greater precarity in terms of housing security (Jennings 2004).

*Figure 1.2* Row houses in Boston's Back Bay neighborhood; bordered to the north by the Charles River and to the south by the Massachusetts Turnpike, the area is home to some of the city's most expensive real estate

Photo by Dan Zuberi

*Figure 1.3* Boston's immigrant and historically working-class neighborhood of North End has been uniquely impacted, first by depressing business activity during years of construction and now by rising property values

Photo by Dan Zuberi

While the Big Dig was plagued with mismanagement during its construction, rapidly increasing property values and gentrified communities is today perhaps its most enduring legacy. Certainly, the Big Dig has made important contributions to the revitalization and livability of downtown Boston. Yet in the broader context of neoliberalism, the benefits have been more mixed for low-income residents, as the economy generates low-wage, non-standard and insecure employment for many—especially the low-skilled and young—and urban regeneration creates increasing rents and soaring housing prices.

Mega-projects remain a fixture of the contemporary urban landscape, which raises important questions about their role in facilitating dislocation, social exclusion and the disenfranchisement of low-income populations. In both Boston and New York City popular—and by many measures highly successful—mega-projects challenge the inclusiveness of contemporary global cities, while at the same time repositioning people and communities in an increasingly globalized economy. An example from New York

City—an icon of economic and social innovation, tenets of a creative and entrepreneurial metropolis—perhaps best epitomizes the transformative potential of mega-projects by design.

## New York City: The High Line

The High Line is a linear public park built atop a former elevated railway—a relic from the New York City's industrial past—running from Gansevoort Street to West 34th Street in lower Manhattan. Once slated for demolition under pressure from the Chelsea Property Owners Group and former tough-on-crime mayor Rudolf Giuliani, today the High Line is widely celebrated as an achievement in grassroots community development and 'green' urban renewal (McGeehan 2011). For many, the High Line epitomizes the *new* New York, a progressive, ecologically sensitive and creative mecca of urban life.

The success of the High Line project has inspired similar reclamation projects in cities across both Canada and the United States. Yet despite its widespread popularity—among visitors and locals alike—questions remain about just who is included in the provision of this ostensibly public space and relatedly how the surrounding community has been transformed as a result? Similar to Boston, whose burgeoning downtown core has attracted a new—and wealthier—demographic, mega-project development in New York has served to reposition the city as a mecca of urban design, high-end consumerism and creative entrepreneurs. An archetype of the neoliberal era, the High Line has contributed to the rising inequality of both economic and cultural resources through the regulation and privatization of public space.

The High Line was born out of the vision of two well-connected West Chelsea residents who, with the creation of a not-for-profit organization called Friends of the High Line, lobbied the City of New York to forgo planned demolition in favor of creating an elevated public park. Working in tandem with local developers and numerous celebrity endorsements, the park touted as an opportunity to revitalize a flagging real estate market through the revitalization of local businesses (McGeehan 2011). Although the West Side of Manhattan was no longer awash in seedy nightclubs, high crime rates and prostitution, the waterfront remained largely off limits to most New Yorkers who saw the High Line as a clear boundary between depravity and the security of Chelsea's burgeoning brownstones (Littke et al. 2015, 3). West Chelsea has itself dramatically altered since the late 1980s when soaring rental prices in the SoHo art district spurred a migration to the area. Cataldi and his collaborators note the role art galleries played in this transformation so that by 1999 the median household income in West Chelsea was upwards of 160 percent of the average for New York City (Cataldi et al. 2011, 375–376).

While former NYC mayor Rudolph Giuliani viewed the High Line as an impediment to crime reduction and a devaluation of commercial property, newly elected mayor Michael Bloomberg perceived the High Line as a flagship opportunity for the city's re-branding—and bid for the 2012 Olympic Games—and in 2005 re-zoned the West Chelsea neighborhood for its development. The third and final phase of the High Line opened in 2014 at a total cost of $240 million. The investment has, according to the Bloomberg Administration, been well worth the public investment, generating an estimated $2 billion in surrounding real estate development (Patrick 2014, 298). In 2010, The Rockefeller Foundation awarded Friends of the High Line founders Joshua David and Robert Hammond the Jane Jacobs Medal in recognition of their creation of a "more diverse, dynamic, and equitable city" (Alvarez & Wright 2012, 2).

Support for the High Line is frequently framed in term of its success as a public space and driver of economic development. The 'value added' can be seen in the transformation of the surrounding West Chelsea and Meatpacking District—by no means impoverished neighborhoods even prior to

*Figure 1.4* Luxury consumerism and rising real estate prices have made NYC one of the most expensive cities to live in North America

Photo by Dan Zuberi

development of the High Line mega-project. However today billboards for luxury brands cater to elite consumers whose growing presence has out-priced multiple generations of small business owners. For example, a *New York Times* op-ed controversially criticized the project for destroying "Gas-oline Ally"—a stretch of family-owned auto-shops along West 29th Street whose rents have reportedly quadrupled (Moss 2012).

In spite of the city's recent economic crisis, real estate prices along the High Line have soared, rising from a median cost of $870,000 to $1,300,000 between October 2008 and June 2009 alone (Cataldi et al. 2011, 377). The mix of art galleries, restaurants and high-end retail spaces parallel to the High Line attract visitors who can enjoy views of the city's recent celeb-rity architectural achievements including work by Frank Gehry and Jean Nouvel. The 2015 opening of the Whitney Museum of American Art at 99 Gansevoort St. is just the latest in infrastructure projects aimed at promoting the area's creative culture. In short, while the High Line was created as a public space promising to engage the entire community, it is simultaneously a product of an already prosperous community; a community made more affluent by the High Line's success. The so-called creative class to which to High Line directly caters now dominates the surrounding community. David Harvey, in 2008, provocatively accused Bloomberg of "turning Manhattan into one vast gated community for the rich" (Harvey 2008, 38).

In addition to the effects on the neighborhoods caused by the High Line development, scholars also note that the High Line itself has been made possible through the regulation and privatization of what is ostensibly pub-lic space. The use of private security guards and the strict enforcement of noise and vendor regulations govern not only who participates in commerce generated by park attendees, but also how the space itself is utilized. Cur-rently only five art venders are permitted to sell on the High Line each day as determined on a first-come-first-serve basis (Loughran 2014, 61). Pro-ponents point to the strategy's success is generating high attendance, while also maintaining low crime rates (Brisman 2012, 381). The inequality of urban public spaces in contemporary cities like New York mirrors neolib-eral principles of competition and entrepreneurialism of which the luxury consumerism and creative capital is front and center.

Significantly, it is not simply the realization of equitable access to urban spaces that neoliberal mega-project developments inhibit. As Bornstein and Leetmaa point out, it is simultaneously the exclusion of urban populations from the planning process and the "uneven distribution of publically created value" neoliberal planning creates (2015, 34). In other words, mega-project developments routinely contribute to the spatial concentration of high-value amenities, which in turn, tend to buttress the uneven valuation of urban land. While studies of mega-project developments have showed that policymakers

*Figure 1.5*  Washington Square Park, located just south of the High Line, has a long
history of anti-gentrification and community activism

Photo by Dan Zuberi

and planners have become increasingly sensitive to public and local community concerns as a way to ensure timely and cost-effective project developments, questions remain about around limitations of more participatory
planning techniques. In the follow section, we explore attempts to influence
or negate neoliberal mega-project developments in San Francisco, CA, and
Montreal, QB. We argue that while these projects fall short of a "just city"
ideal, they provide important insight into the politics of planning and the
growing import and power of citizen engagement.

## San Francisco, CA: Bayview/Hunters Point
## Redevelopment

While neoliberal urban renewal is gentrifying many cities across North
America, San Francisco is perhaps one of the most gentrified cities on either
side of the U.S.–Canada border. Facilitated largely by an influx of tech companies and creative startups, San Francisco now boasts a luxury market well

*Figure 1.6* Downtown San Francisco skyline puts the city's wealth on display
Photo by Dan Zuberi

beyond the financial means of many residents. The average San Francisco housing unit now sells for approximately $800,000. At the same time, a shrinking middle class and rising homeless population has helped produce a significant demographic shift amongst the resident population. Scholars now point to San Francisco as an example of 'super-gentrification', a term employed to highlight the scale and intensity of social-spatial dislocation experienced by many of the city's residents (Cohen & Martí 2009, 425). Driven by the auspiciousness of 'smart growth' planning, which includes in-fill development to limit urban sprawl and promote environmental sustainability, urban planners have also faced increasing pressure to ensure affordability and engage communities impacted by mega-development.

Bayview/Hunters Point (BVHP) is a Redevelopment Area located in the southeastern corner of San Francisco, directly south of and adjacent to Candlestick Park, San Francisco's main sports stadium from 1960 to 2013. The area also includes the former Hunters Point Naval Shipyard as well as the city's largest low-income housing project. The neighborhood has a long history of ethnic diversity as thousands of immigrants and African Americans migrated to BVHP for work and affordable rents (Ellen et al. 2011, 236). Once referred to as Butchertown or Putrid Row due to the prevalence of

*Figure 1.7* A U.S. Navy ship docked in San Francisco Bay
Photo by Dan Zuberi

nineteenth-century slaughterhouses, in the mid-twentieth century, the U.S. Navy began using the area to study and dispose of nuclear waste. Closed in 1974, the area is now a federally funded brownfield site due to high levels of chemical ground and water contamination. Studies conducted by the San Francisco Health Department show residents of Bayview/Hunters Point experience elevated rates of asthma, diabetes and cancer. They are also routinely among the most impoverished families citywide (Metzger & Lendvay 2006, 104–107).

Together Bayview/Hunters Point and Candlestick Park span over 700 acres and have long been slated for large-scale redevelopment. The Lennar Corporation plans to construct a new sports stadium, 3,700 square feet of commercial and retail space, 10,500 residential units, an 8,000-square-foot arena, and 336 acres of waterfront parkway. Proponents argue the project will provide much needed infrastructure and services (including improved transit) as well as jobs to the surrounding community, while critics remain concerned about future displacement and further environmental contamination. Even prior to construction, the Bayview/Hunters Point project has already been recognized in 2011 by the Brookings Institute as one of three 'Transformative Investments in the United States.' The award along with numerous others from the American Planning Association, the World Architecture Festival and the Pacific Coast Builders, have all served to stimulate private sector interest and support for the project (Dillon 2014, 1210).

However, despite considerable support among industry proponents and politicians, many local residents raised concerns about the project's potential impact. In the face of mounting public opposition and an ordinance for a citywide referendum on the fate of the project, the Lennar Corporation—the project's main developer—agreed to approve a Community Benefits Agreement (CBA) in exchange for the project's endorsement in 2008. The San Francisco Labor Council, the Alliance of Californians for Community Empowerment (a non-profit organization), and the San Francisco Organizing Project (a coalition of faith-based groups), collectively known as the Alliance for District 10, agreed to support the project in exchange for 32 percent of units being reserved for low-income housing in addition to $37.5 million in community funding.

While environmental concerns were not included in the CBA, the California Environmental Impact (EI) assessment process, in tandem with the City of San Francisco's land-use policies, resulted in additional community benefits such as a health and well-being center, a workforce development program, and financing for educational programming (Bornstein & Leetmaa 2015, 37). While the results of the EI process remains subject to public oversight, the CBA signed between Lennar and the Alliance for District 10 remains private with decisions on spending made by a seven-member committee.

Unfortunately, according to some reports, the Bayview/Hunters Point and Candlestick Park CBA has been plagued by dysfunction, and the Implementation Committee has failed to spend the vast majority of funds. The single chair reserved for a community member at-large has been vacant for nearly 2 years, while representatives from Lennar, the Alliance for District 10, and various other development bodies have consistently failed to compromise. Moreover, Lennar withdrew $30 million of the $37.5 million outlined in the CBA citing years-long project delays. And while upwards of $7 million USD remain allocated for community improvement grants, a mere $1.4 million have been spent (Green 2015). While the Alliance for District 10 may have succeeded securing funding for community initiatives in an effort to limit the impact of gentrification, critics argue the organization does not adequately represent the Bayview/Hunters Point community who continue to be shut out of the decision-making process. Without adequate oversight or regulation, the implementation process now suffers from a lack of transparency and decreasing public legitimacy.

The CBA compromise reached in the development of Bayview/Hunters Point and Candlestick Park represent what Cohen and Martí refer to as the "'sweet spot' between the interests of private sector gentrification-inducing development and preservation of an equitable, diverse, politically progressive city" (2009, 444). However, as the challenges experienced by the Implementation Committee reveal, questions remain about the ability of such a mutually accommodating strategy to adequate support equitable or just development policies. When communities remain underrepresented and CBAs are not subject to public oversight or regulation, there are few mechanisms to ensure accountability or transparency. And while CBAs certainly represent an important and increasingly popular tool of urban regeneration, more work must be done to ensure that their outcomes remain equitable and representative of community needs.

## Montreal, QC: Point St. Charles

While CBAs or other forms of community consultation and cooperation are increasingly common in mega-project development processes, sometimes opposition from community groups is fervent and compromise becomes increasingly unachievable. However, the outright rejection, or substantive modification, of proposed mega-project development is made more difficult in the context of neoliberal economic restructuring and the pressure to foster globally competitive cities. In Canada, the hosting of international sporting events and improvements for the benefit of the tourism industry has driven much mega-project development. Some recent examples include the 2010 Winter Olympics in Vancouver, the 2015 Pan Am Games in Toronto, and a proposal for a new $890 million sports stadium in Calgary (which is also currently putting together a bid for the 2026 summer Olympic games). Unlike the case of San Francisco, in Canada companies typically do not employ CBAs and instead, "recent efforts to expand the community benefits exacted from or associated with large-scale urban development projects have largely fallen within government defined and driven processes" (Bornstein & Leetmaa 2015, 39). While city governments in both Canada and the United States certainly remain constrained by fiscal shortages and increasingly concerned with attracting private investment, they also remain publicly accountable to urban citizens.

Montreal is Canada's second largest city and has long been a national hub of arts and culture as well as civic activism. Protests and organized opposition to mega-project development has routinely thwarted both public and private plans for the construction of new highways, condo towers and tourism facilities. Negotiation has also at times led to enhanced opportunities for community participation, while political pressure in the form of protests, petitions and public outcry have also "contributed to or been blamed for the collapse of redevelopment initiatives" (Bornstein 2007, 5). In short, mega-project development in Montreal has long been highly politicized, and recent efforts to construct a large-scale billion-dollar entertainment complex adjacent to the city's downtown have been no exception.

In 2005, Loto-Québec (a crown corporation responsible for development and regulation of gaming in the province of Québec) and local performance export Cirque du Soleil announced plans to construct a massive entertainment complex in the du Harvre area of Montreal. The plans included a flagship 2,500-seat theater to host Cirque Du Soleil and visiting performances, a 300-room hotel, and adjacent park space in which circus tents and an artists' wharf could host visitors. Loto-Québec also announced plans for a new casino and exhibition center. Despite promises of over 6,000 new jobs and a substantial influx of capital to both the city and immediate community, fervent opposition quickly emerged.

Located on the southern fringe of Montreal's downtown, the Pointe St. Charles neighborhood, directly adjacent to the proposed project site, is one of the city's poorest areas made up of predominantly working- and lower-class families who felt the proposed development did not serve the immediate needs of their community. Residents raised concerns around the ongoing affordability of housing, provision of social services, and potentially deleterious socioeconomic impacts associated with high numbers of visitors to an entertainment venue (CBC News 2006). In Canada, gambling is highly regulated by provincial governments that limit both the forms and associated products available to gaming customers. In this way, the proposed partnership between Loto-Québec and Cirque du Soleil worked to open the door to a free market model for gambling, in addition to moving the city's existing casino from its currently more isolated location into downtown in an effort to attract new visitors.

In response to these critiques, Loto-Québec and Cirque du Soleil promised Point St. Charles residents preferential hiring and job training at the casino complex. Additional funding was announced for the creation of an addiction awareness campaign and increased public consultation (Pertiz 2009). However, after a special committee convened to assess the development recommended the government suspend the project for 18 months in order to complete further impact studies and public participation, opposition had become insurmountable. Protests, petitions and public outcry from organizations such as the Welfare Rights Committee and Action Gardien de Pointe St-Charle (a coalition of community groups and residents) succeeded in eroding political support for the project, while at the same time drawing renewed attention to the needs to low-income communities.

While proponents of the project criticized opponents for their unwillingness to compromise and pointed to the loss of valuable jobs for local residents, the success of community groups in garnering popular and political support for their concerns remains significant. Despite efforts to discredit public input into mega-project development, the city of Montreal chose to listen to the concerns of residents, and through a public evaluation found the potential harm the project posed outweighed even substantive projected financial gain. This case serves as an important counter-example to the dominant trend of mega-project displacement, while at the same time lending support to the realization of 'just city' alternatives. Effective mobilizing can block or force major revisions to proposed development, but it also requires substantive political will to hold public officials accountable to community demands.

Taken together the experience of Point St. Charles, Montreal and Bayview/Hunters Point, San Francisco suggest that mega-project development is perhaps not inevitably displacing. It is the all-to-frequent lack of public transparency, accountability and willingness to cooperate and even compensate impacted communities, particularly those most vulnerable to the pressures of gentrification, that continues to characterize mega-project regeneration in the contemporary era.

## Conclusion

Mega-project developments such as the Boston's Big Dig and NYC's High Line illustrate how issues of access, privilege, economic growth and consumption are bound up in the neoliberalization of large-scale public infrastructure projects. As Littke and his collaborators point out, the influence of flagship mega-project developments such as those chronicled in this chapter "raises questions of who is initiating the provision of public space, who public space is intended for, and what consequences a project of this magnitude can have for the surrounding locale" (Littke et al. 2015, 2). As neoliberal policies and practices continue to shape the nature of mega-project development and who is included in the design and approval of these initiatives, direct and indirect dislocation and displacement emerges from successful projects. Promoting the livability of urban communities means confronting the dislocation and homogenization that stems from neoliberal mega-project design and taking steps to mitigate this harm. The examples Boston and New York City serve as important illustrations of the socio-spatial consequences of mega-project developments that fail to adequately respond to or consider lower-income communities. In the examples from San Francisco and Montreal, low-income populations have mobilized and taken center stage in both the negotiation, reshaping and rejection of mega-project developments, which in turn help to highlight the ongoing importance of local political will in the realization of just city alternatives. In the following chapter, we turn to issues of social housing and the political will required to support the fundamental right to shelter. We explore how competitive city planning and creative class consumerism has helped to redefine the social-spatial distribution of poverty in both Canada and the United State, albeit through radically different approaches to low-income housing. Just as mega-project development has been subject to public pressure to ensure accountability and public participation, social housing initiatives have emerged as important spaces for debate about the nature of density and the communal urban life it facilitates.

## Notes

1 See the "Ungentry Project" for an interactive map of housing, poverty and other demographic statistics in downtown Boston over time. http://codeforboston. github.io/ungentry/ [last accessed 13 March 2017].
2 See "Affordable Housing" by the *University of Massachusetts Boston* for housing rates. www.umb.edu/life_on_campus/housing/affordinghousing [last accessed 13 March 2017].

## References

Altshuler, A.A., and Luberoff, D.E. (2003) *Mega-Projects: The Changing Politics of Urban Public Investment*. New York: Brookings Institution Press.
Alvarez, A., and Wright, M. (2012) "New York City's High Line: Participatory Planning or Gentrification?", Working Paper, The Pennsylvania State University. http://forms.gradsch.psu.edu/diversity/mcnair/mcnair_jrnl2012_14/files/2012-Alvarez.pdf [last accessed 13 March 2017].
Bearfield, D. and Dubnick, M. (2007) "Sowing and Reaping at the Big Dig: The Legacies of Neomanagerialism", *Administrative Theory and Praxis*, 29(1): 132–139.
Bornstein, L. (2007) "Community Responses to Mega Project Development", www.mcgill.ca/urbanplanning/files/urbanplanning/RR07-01E-bornstein.pdf
Bornstein, L., and Leetmaa, K. (2015) "Moving beyond Indignation: Stakeholder Tactics, Legal Tools and Community Benefits in Large-Scale Redevelopment Projects", *Oñati Socio-Legal Series*, 5: 29–50.
Brenner, N., and Theodore, N. (2002) "Cities and Geographies of 'Actually Existing Neoliberalism'", *Antipode*, 34(3): 349–379.
Brisman, A. (2012) "An Elevated Challenge to 'Broken Windows': The High Line (New York)", *Crime, Media, and Culture*, 8(3): 381.
Bushouse, B. (2002) "Changes in Mitigation: Comparing Boston's Big Dig and 1950s Urban Renewal", *Public Works Management Policy Journal*, 7: 52–62.
Cataldi, M., Kelley, D., Zuzmich, H., Maier-Rothe, J., and Tang, J. (2011) "Residues of a Dream World: The High Line, 2011", *Theory, Culture, and Society*, 28(7–8): 358–389.
CBC News. (2006) "Tremblay Slammed for Supporting Casino Move", *Canadian Broadcasting Corporation*. Published 28 February 2006. www.cbc.ca/news/

canada/montreal/tremblay-slammed-for-supporting-casino-move-1.583790 [last accessed 13 March 2017].

Clarke, S.E., and Gaile, G.L. (1992) "The New Wave: Postfederal Local Economic Development Strategies", *Economic Development Quarterly*, 6(2): 187–198.

Cohen, P., and Martí, F. (2009) "Searching for the 'Sweet Spot' in San Francisco", In L. Porter and K. Shaw (eds.), *Whose Urban Renaissance: An International Comparison of Urban Regeneration Strategies*. Abingdon: Routledge. Pp. 424–454.

Ellen, J., Schwartz, S.L., and Austin, M.J. (2011) "The Bayview Hunters Point Foundation for Community Improvement: A Pioneering Multi-Ethnic Human Service Organization (1971–2008)", *Journal of Evidence-Based Social Work*, 8(1–2): 235–252.

Fainstein, S. (2008) "Mega-Projects in New York, London and Amsterdam", *International Journal of Urban and Regional Research*, 32(4): 768–785.

Fein, M.R. (2012) "Tunnel Vision: 'Invisible' Highways and Boston's 'Big Dig' in the Age of Privatization", *Journal of Planning History*, 11: 47–69.

Gelinas, N. (2007) "Lessons of Boston's Big Dig", *City Journal*. www.city-journal. org/html/lessons-boston's-big-dig-13049.html [last accessed 13 March 2017].

Gellert, P.K., and Lynch, B.D. (2003) "Mega-Projects as Displacements", *International Social Science Journal*, 55(175): 15–25.

Green, E. (2015) "Infighting Ties Up Millions in Bayview-Hunters Point Grants", *San Francisco Chronicle*. Published 25 July 2015. www.sfchronicle.com/news/ article/Infighting-ties-up-millions-in-Bayview-Hunters-6405729.php [last accessed 13 March 2017].

Harvey, D. (2008) "The Right to the City", *The New Left Review*, 53: 23–40.

Hellman, D., Schachter, G., Sum, A., Ziparo, A., and Zoppi, C. (1997) "The Impact of Mega-Infrastructure Projects on Urban Development: Boston and the Messina Straits", *European Planning Series*, 5: 109–123.

Jennings, J. (2004) "Urban Planning, Community Participation, and the Roxbury Master Plan in Boston", *ANNALS*, 594: 12–33.

Jonas, A.E.G., and McCarthy, L. (2010) "Redevelopment at All Costs? A Critical Review and Examination of the American Model of Urban Management and Regeneration", In J. Diamond, J. Liddle, A. Southern, and P. Osei (eds.), *Urban Regeneration Management: International Perspectives*. New York, NY: Routledge. Pp. 31–62.

Kadi, J., and Musterd, S. (2014) "Housing for the Poor in the Neo-Liberalizing Just City: Still Affordable But Increasingly Inaccessible", *Journal of Economic and Social Geography*, 106(3): 246–262.

Lehrer, U., and Laidley, J. (2008) "Old Mega-Projects Newly Packaged? Waterfront Redevelopment in Toronto", *International Journal of Urban and Regional Research*, 32(4): 783–803.

Littke, H., Locke, R., and Haas, T. (2015) "Taking the High Line: Elevated Parks, Transforming Neighbourhoods, and the Ever-Changing Relationship between the Urban Nature", *Journal of Urbanism*. DOI: 10.1080/17549175.2015.1063532

Loughran, K. (2014) "Parks for Profit: The High Line, Growth Machines, and the Uneven Development of Urban Public Spaces", *City and Community*, 13: 49–68.

McGeehan, P. (2011) "The High Line Isn't Just a Sight to See; It's Also an Economic Dynamo", *The New York Times*. Published 5 June 2011. www.nytimes. com/2011/06/06/nyregion/with-next-phase-ready-area-around-high-line-is-flourishing.html?_r=5&src=me&ref=nyregion [last accessed 13 March 2017].

Metzger, E.S., and Lendvay, J.M. (2006) "Commentary: Seeking Environmental Justice through Public Participation: A Community-Based Water Quality Assessment in Bayview Hunters Point", *Environmental Practice*, 8(2): 104–114.

Moss, J. (2012) "Disney World on the Hudson" *The New York Times*. Published 21 August 2012. www.nytimes.com/2012/08/22/opinion/in-the-shadows-of-the-high-line.html [last accessed 13 March 2017].

Orueta, F.D., and Fainstein, S. (2008) "The New Mega-Projects: Genesis and Impacts", *International Journal of Urban and Regional Research*, 32(4): 759–767.

Patrick, D.J. (2014) "A Matter of Displacement: A Queer Urban Ecology of New York City's High Line", *Social and Cultural Geography*, 15(8): 920–941.

Pertiz, I. (2009) "Montrealers Considering Role of the Dice in Their City", *The Globe and Mail*. Published 9 April 2009. www.theglobeandmail.com/news/national/montrealers-considering-role-of-the-dice-in-their-city/article24356681/ [last accessed 13 March 2017].

Robinson, J. (2008) "Crime and Regeneration in Urban Communities: The Case of the Big Dig in Boston, Massachusetts", *Built Environment*, 34: 46–61.

Siemiatycki, M. (2013) "Riding the Wave: Explaining Cycles in Urban Mega-Project Development", *Journal of Economic Policy Reform*, 16(2): 160–178.

Tajima, K. (2003) "New Estimates for the Demand for Urban Green Space: Implications for Valuing the Environmental Benefits of Boston's Big Dig Project", *Journal of Urban Affairs*, 25(5): 641–655.

Young, A.H. (1984) "Urban Development Action Grants: The New Orleans Experience", *Public Administration Quarterly*, 8: 112–129.

# 2 Urban Renewal in North America Today
## From HOPE VI to New Models of Inclusive Urban Redevelopment

The roots of urban renewal policies in North America can be traced to the 1949 and 1954 United States Housing Acts. Under the purview of the Truman Administration, federal funds were earmarked to municipal efforts to clear slums in order to attract private commercial investment. Seen as a source of social dysfunction and a 'blight' on metropolitan economies, low-income neighborhoods were bulldozed on mass. The destruction of public housing and the forceful removal of largely black inner-city communities transformed the American postwar social and economic urban landscape through the public sanctioning of private development. Working-class neighborhoods were largely destroyed, reinforcing racial segregation and socio-spatial inequality (Thomas & Hwang 2003, 10–11). By the time the program ended in 1974, $53 billion in federal funds had been spent on more than 2,100 projects nationwide (U.S. Department of Housing and Urban Development 1974, 15).

In Canada, urban renewal strategies mirrored those introduced in the United States with the signing of the 1957 National Housing Act. Slum clearances and the leveling of infrastructure across Canadian cities ensued, and over the following decade, the Canadian Mortgage and Housing Corporation—a crown company—funded 37 urban renewal initiatives nationwide (Verbeek 2012, 7). While not nearly as extensive as urban renewal projects in the United States, the stigmatization of urban poverty in Canada remained. In both countries, postwar urban renewal programs sought to combat social malaise through economic revitalization and demographic displacement.

In the late 1950s and early 1960s, as manufacturing declined and suburbanization continued to expand, cities employed urban renewal funding to construct middle-class residential alternatives in a bid to revitalize the urban core. New York's Manhattan Plaza, Boston's West End, Detroit's Lafayette Village, San Francisco's Golden Gateway Center, and Los Angeles's Bunk Hill Towers are just a few examples of U.S. efforts to renew urban areas.

In Canada Ottawa's LeBreton Flats, Vancouver's Shaughnessy Heights, and Halifax's Scotia Square all exemplify similar postwar urban renewal projects (Picton 2010; Wade 1994; Verbeek 2012). Each of these housing developments radically transformed the North American postwar urban landscape and produced new patterns of social-spatial inequality. While federal funding continued to drive urban regeneration initiatives, by the late 1960s, political support for federal housing subsidies, particularly in the United States, had all but evaporated (see Birch 2012).

Mounting costs of American military operations in Vietnam, escalating civil unrest at home and a declining Fordist economy—all in the context of renewed political conservatism—diminished support for federally funded urban redevelopment, particularly for low-income housing in the United States. In Canada, the federally funded high-rise residential development projects of the 1960s were quickly stalled with an amendment to the National Housing Act in 1973. Federal support for social housing was terminated altogether just a few years later when responsibility was delegated to provincial governments (Bacher 1993, 211–213). Businesses relocated to suburban centers or simply moved operations overseas leaving urban centers with limited capital. In the United States, the shift away from project-based subsidized housing and toward a voucher-based program of individualized need began slowly in the 1970s, becoming the norm under the devolution policies of the Reagan and Bush Administrations (Fraser et al. 2012, 2013; Thomas & Hwang 2003, 10–11). In the process of conversion to a voucher-based system of allocation, scholars estimate that more than a quarter-million units of low-income housing were lost across the United States (DeFilippis & Wyly 2008).

Over time, a shift has occurred among policymakers and scholars away from tackling the causes of concentrated urban poverty and toward the pathologization of those individuals living in poverty. A consequence of mounting conservatism during the 1970s and 1980s, poverty became increasingly associated with drugs and drug-related crime, particularly in the urban United States. A widespread 'moral panic' among middle- and upper-class populations subsequently called for new mechanisms to address urban poverty (Goetz 2000, 160). Mass decentralization initiatives ensued. Across the United States, federal programming including Moving to Opportunity and HOPE VI were championed as the solution to urban blight. In Canada, the strategy of mixed-income social housing came under fire during the late 1980s with the election of a conservative federal government, and housing policies were devolved to provincial (and in some cases municipal) authorities.

In this chapter, we explore the logic of decentralized poverty alleviation initiatives and examine their impact on low-income communities.

*Figure 2.1* The residential towers of St. James Town, Toronto, were first built in the 1960s to accommodate the city's rapid population growth

Photo by Dan Zuberi

Contemporary trends in urban social-spatial inequality across North America are the legacy of postwar urban renewal projects, but are also sustained by the ongoing stigmatization of urban poverty. The shift from postwar demolition and relocation to mixed-income and high-density urban communities is explored through the HOPE VI program in the United States and in Canada's Regent Park. The former is a federal program that grants cities financial capital to develop depressed social housing across the United States. While no comparable federal-level program exists in Canada, Regent Park, located in downtown Toronto, has recently experienced the largest redevelopment of social housing to mixed-tenure in Canadian history.

We argue that despite evidence that calls into question the benefits of mixed-income neighborhoods for impoverished individuals, the sociological assumptions underscoring their promotion continue to drive urban design. We find that even the introduction of more participatory and inclusive planning practices, such as those pioneered in Seattle, WA, have difficulty overcoming pressures associated with heightened growth and gentrification. In pursuit of a more Just City model of urban life, participatory practices must be augmented by a political commitment to foster more equitable and affordable urban communities.

## Mixed Communities in the Contemporary Urban Landscape

Since the early 1990s, governments on both sides of the Canada–U.S. border have reinvigorated city centers through widespread deregulation of private business and the funding of significant infrastructure projects through public–private partnerships. At the turn of the century, individuals began to re-occupy city centers on mass, drawn to lower living costs and burgeoning amenities (Birch 2012, 128). The fostering of a 24-hour downtown in many North American cities helped to reinvigorate urban economies, largely fueled by a young entrepreneurial and creative class of young, single adults with higher rates of both education and disposable income than their predecessors. While in 1970 children and the elderly accounted for more than one-third of downtown residents across the United States, today adults between the ages 18 and 34 make up nearly half the urban population (45 percent); the majority of whom are also White (Birch 2012, 138–139). While the demographics of urban neighborhoods have certainly changed, so too have their aesthetic and design.

Twenty-first-century urban renewal touts mixed communities—in both use and occupancy—that work to attract valuable consumers and discipline anti-social behavior (Flint 2006). Informed largely by the work of Wilson and Kelling (1982), policymakers have increasingly sought to curb crime rates by cracking down on signs of disorder such as graffiti and vandalism. Public housing has been particularly targeted resulting in an increased police presence, and the introduction of federal initiatives including the U.S. Public Housing Drug Elimination Program and the One-Strike You're Out policy (Ireland et al. 2006, 301–302). Moreover, the privatization of public spaces, including parks and promenades, have also worked to regulate life in urban cores, transforming spaces once associated with the formation of social capital into liabilities and untapped sources of profit in an evolving marketplace (Madanipour 2010). In short, the shift toward mixed communities and the regulation of urban space "reflects a fundamental change in social thinking about how best to combat poverty and help underprivileged populations" (Clark 2008, 515). Unlike previous efforts at relocation via segregation, today scholars and policymakers alike promote the integration of mixed-income populations; collectively they assume that such efforts will produce more livable and sustainable communities.

The empirical data supporting the social and economic benefits of integration however remains ambiguous (Clark 2008; Ellen & Turner 1997).

Figure 2.2 The original low-rises of Toronto's Regent Park have long been considered a 'blight' on an otherwise burgeoning downtown area

Photo by Dan Zuberi

While social housing blocks have traditionally been associated with higher crime rates, including those related to drug trafficking and consumption, many residents also report a wide range of benefits derived from communal living (Axtell & Tooley 2015; August 2014). Without ignoring the real problems that exist with social housing developments on both sides of the Canada–U.S. border, we join those scholars who argue for a more nuanced perspective on the effects of low-income residency (August & Walks 2012; James 2010; Laakso 2013; DeFilippis & Wyly 2008). In the context of decreased funding for social housing, advocates of social mix continue to argue that private sector investment in depressed neighborhoods not only physically revitalizes communities badly in need of investment, but also improves the life chances of low-income residents. Critics however contend that this perspective legitimizes what is in fact a false choice between ongoing neglect of low-income communities and their all but inevitable gentrification (August 2014; DeFilippis 2004; Slater 2006).

## Neighborhood Effects

While the residential mobility initiatives of the late 1960s and early 1970s were aimed at reducing racial segregation and providing housing on mass, the current social housing program is designed to mitigate the effects of concentrated poverty. The crime, social insecurity and behavioral pathologies associated with high degrees of concentrated poverty have produced a tenuous scenario whereby middle-class communities fear their proximity to low-income individuals who, in turn, are left isolated and stigmatized in an increasingly exclusive urban core. According to Van Ham et al.:

> A vast literature on neighborhood effects culminated in the idea that living in deprived neighbourhoods has a negative effect on residents' life chances over and above the effect of their individual characteristics. Neighborhood effects have been reported on outcomes such as educational achievement, school dropout rates, deviant behavior, social exclusion, health, transition rates from welfare to work, and social and occupational mobility.
>
> (Van Ham et al. 2012, 1)

Largely informed by the work of William Julius Wilson (1987, 1996) who argued low-income individuals "cannot be understood independently of the macro social and economic forces which shape them", according to Wilson, high-poverty neighborhoods would eventually suffer from disintegration and 'ghetto-related behaviors' including criminality, gang violence and dysfunctional family structures. This depiction of low-income urban areas mirrored that of James Wilson and George Kelling (1982) whose broken windows theory promoted zero-tolerance policies for combatting crime. Popularized by municipal leaders including former NYC mayor Rudy Giuliani and NYC police commissioner William Bratton, tough on crime policing of urban areas has led to the direct targeting of activities such as squeegeeing, panhandling and petty theft. Like the deterministic claims associated with neighborhood effects scholarship, Wilson and Kelling saw low-income neighborhoods as breeding grounds for more serious crime. The idea of neighborhood effects has sometimes been closely associated with a focus on the relationship between values and norms of urban minority communities, and social and economic marginality.

The perceived benefits of functionally and socially mixed urban communities have driven the mass-scale redevelopment of urban housing across the United States and more recently transformed Canada's oldest and largest social housing development, Regent Park. Gentrification of existing working-class communities through the integration of low-income individuals within middle- and upper-middle class housing developments seeks to transform the deviance of poverty through its deconcentration. However, as the experience of many low-income residents reveals, the widespread policy assumptions associated with mixed communities lacks strong supporting evidence. Instead, projects like HOPE VI and Regent Park have been pursued at the expense of important social networks and other sources of social capital. In the context of neoliberal urban governance and competitive city modeling, a normative consensus among policymakers not only privileges a particular social, racial and class-based pathology, but also prioritizes consumption and entrepreneurship over and above commitments to social justice and security.

In what follows, we explore two of the largest social housing redevelopment projects in North America: HOPE VI and Regent Park. While in many ways distinct—in geography, financing and scope—both provide an important window into the social implications of neoliberal planning policies. In the context of entrepreneurial-inspired urban design, the privatization of public housing through its mixed-use redevelopment reveals one strategy in which urban regeneration is transforming life in urban cores.

## Social Housing Reform

HOPE VI was born out of the National Commission on Severely Distressed Public Housing and the Housing and Urban Development Reform Act of 1989, which together sought to address the 'severely distressed' state of 86,000 (of a total of 1.3 million) public housing units across the United States. In 1992, the U.S. Congress introduced HOPE VI, a nationwide program aimed at transforming the physical, managerial and social services of public housing blocks in a bid to make residents more self-reliant. Housing authorities were invited to submit proposals for developments of up to 500 units and for projects of up to $50 million. Inspired by the success of mixed-housing strategies undertaken in Boston, MA, U.S. policymakers promoted the revitalization of existing public housing complexes through public–private partnerships in an effort to attract middle-income residents.

The widespread demolition of existing public housing blocks meant residents were forced to relocate as many of their homes were leveled and eventually rebuilt. However, one-to-one replacement of subsidized housing was not guaranteed, and new developments hosted only a minimal percentage of units reserved for low-income individuals and families. While many families were given vouchers in order to secure alternative living arrangement, evidence suggests that many individuals simply remained in the surrounding area or moved to areas even more depressed by income (Trudeau 2006; Goetz 2010). While the promotion of mixed-income neighborhoods—the cornerstone of the HOPE VI program—varied across the more than 200 projects funded by HOPE VI grants between 1993 and 2010, each conform to a strategy that attempts to combat poverty by helping low-income people live in closer proximity to wealthier families (Fraser et al. 2013, 523; Laakso 2013, 30). In short, HOPE VI resulted in the relocation of tens of thousands of the nation's public housing residents (Axtell & Tooley 2015, 279) whose new zip codes were seen as integral to social reform.

In Canada, no equivalent federal-level program currently exists for low-income housing, the responsibility for which was devolved to provincial governments during the 1990s. In the case of Ontario, home to Canada's largest city of Toronto, housing policy was further devolved to the municipal level in 2000. Facing significant financial constraints, the City of Toronto introduced new governance structures on all social housing programs, requiring them to become more entrepreneurial in their fiscal management and delivery of services (August & Walks 2012, 276). It is within this context that the country's largest and oldest public housing project, Regent Park, was in 2005 slated for substantive redevelopment.

First built in the 1940s and early 1950s in the tradition of 'Garden City' design, Regent Park is comprised of a series of low and high-rise apartment blocks located within Toronto's downtown core. Surrounded by commercial shopping districts and high-income single-family homes, Regent Park has long been considered a blight in an otherwise burgeoning area. After decades of neglect, in 2005, the City of Toronto partnered with a private developer on the Regent Park Revitalization Plan, a 12-year, $1 billion mixed-income redevelopment. Formally home to approximately 7,600 residents in 2,087 subsidized units, once complete 69 acres of land will provide housing for 12,500 people in 5,115 units—approximately 2,000 of which are to be designated as low income. In short, a three-fold increase in density will reduce what was originally a community of exclusively subsidized homes to one in which a minority of just 26 percent will remain (August 2014, 1317).

Despite being inspired by the experience of HOPE VI in the United States, significant differences distinguish Regent Park redevelopment plan. In addition to lacking any federal funding for social housing in Canada, no tenant-based

*Figure 2.3* Toronto's redeveloped Regent Park towers
Photo by Dan Zuberi

subsidies currently exist. In other words, unlike the HOPE VI model, which relies on vouchers for tenant relocation, in Canada subsidies are determined by income level. Moreover, a requirement that all pre-existing units be replaced at a one-to-one ratio has resulted in a substantial increase in density in order for market housing to be constructed. The result has been that while all former residents are given the right to return, they will return to a social setting radically different than before. And while the logic of social mix prescribes heightened levels of integration to improve life chances, critics argue that inequality persists largely through the ongoing stigmatization and marginalization of low-income residents (August 2014; August & Walks 2012).

Much like HOPE VI, in Regent Park "revitalization is guided, to a significant extent, by a concern with the moral regulation of poor and working-class city-dwellers (particularly those who are new Canadians and/or racialized minorities) by altering the built environment in which they live" (James 2010, 70). The deviance and criminalization of poverty associated with Regent Park residents has been well documented by Purdy (2005, 2003) who has helped to expose how decades of negative media publicity contributed to the rampant stigmatization of the area. While Regent Park residents now benefit from improved amenities such as recreation facilities, a cultural center and new retail services, the sociological benefits of social mix are less clear.

While both proponents and critics of the revitalization project agree that infrastructure improvements are both desirable and necessary, many scholars continue to argue that social mix does not adequately address many of underlying structural determinants of poverty: namely inadequate investments in social services, job creation and educational resources (August 2014; Lees 2014; Slater 2006; DeFilippis 2004). In other words, the individualization of poverty and the pathological behavior it ostensibly contributes to can ignore the political and economic policies that are deeply implicated in its creation.

There is in fact a clear link between theories of neighborhood effects and broken windows and the practice of mass-scale urban renewal exemplified by HOPE VI (Musterd & Andersson 2005). A consensus around the relationship between poverty and social pathologies including criminality and dysfunction has worked to justify the destruction of over 100,000 public housing units across the United States. While some low-income families have been able to re-enter public housing units using vouchers for mixed-income communities, one-to-one replacement of low-income units was not part of the HOPE VI model, which resulted in the widespread dislocation of low-income families. Scholars have long documented the significant residential instability resulting from HOPE VI projects, including a redistribution of neighborhood poverty as families relocated to even poorer and racially segregated areas (Goetz 2003; Keels et al. 2005)

HOPE VI promised that by generating market choice—through the introduction of private units into a public sector housing projects—low-income individuals would make significant fiscal gains. Stimulating private investment into depressed urban neighborhoods would provide impoverished populations access to improved goods and services and new forms of employment. Most importantly, HOPE VI aimed to provide role models and resource-rich social networks to residents whose poverty was seen as the result of dysfunctional behavior and social isolation. While a number of studies have found HOPE VI communities to be potentially safer and freer of crime than their social housing predecessors, other improvements—in income, educational achievements, and health—are less clear (Lens 2014; Popkin et al. 2012; Ireland et al. 2006; Keene & Geronimus 2011; Lipman 2011). A degree of consensus does suggest that neighborhood conditions may play a role in shaping individual outcomes, however determining which characteristics impact which outcomes or type of family is far from clear. In short, major empirical, methodological and normative questions remain (Ellen & Turner 1997, 833; Bauder 2002).

While longitudinal and empirical studies continue to drive policy debates over the benefits of mixed living, there are also important normative implications associated with the HOPE VI program. For example, Bauder points out that "the idea of neighbourhood effects can be interpreted as yet another episode in the on-going discourse of inner-city marginality that blames marginal communities for their own misery" (2002, 88). He goes on to suggest that programs like HOPE VI are built on assumptions of universal standards—in childrearing, educational achievement and employment success—that are not representative of all communities. Musterd and Andersson (2005) also note that housing segregation is often most pronounced for upper-income earners whose concentration and isolation are rarely at issue. In short, these authors call attention to the pathology of urban poverty whereby middle- and upper-income earners have little to gain by social mixing. Moreover, studies suggest that low-income residents of mixed-income developments like those funded by HOPE VI face a wide array of obstacles to integration.

Fostering cross-class ties and new social networks is not as straightforward or natural as much of the neighborhood effects literature suggests. Ethnographic studies find that social mixing rarely crosses racial, ethnic or class lines and that high degrees of animosity can develop between more affluent residents who have purchased units at market rates and low-income residents subsidized by voucher or other subsidy programs (Fraser et al. 2013; Freeman 2006). Landlords and site managers may further alienate low-income residents by assigning them lower status in the community because they pay less to be a member (Fraser et al. 2012). Kipfer and Petrunia (2009) suggest that demands to attract enough middle-income residents to offset the cost of subsidies can result in intensified surveillance and discipline of low-income residents, particularly in the context of shared public space. As a result, "relocation often results in increased social isolation and increased vulnerability from the loss of coping strategies derived from place-based social capital" (Axtell & Tooley 2015, 281). Networks of material and emotional support, built over time and with considerable levels of inter-personal trust, Putnam argues, are paramount to fostering vibrant and secure communities, but are increasingly absent from many American cities (Putnam 1995).

Despite the obvious upgrade in the physical infrastructure and environment post redevelopment, it remains is unclear to what extent low-income populations benefit from the mixed-income neighborhoods promoted by HOPE VI or Regent Park. A breakdown of social networks may leave some lower-income people isolated, lacking material and emotional support in a highly stressful and new environment. Alternatively, even when individuals return to the area, the degree of social transformation brought on by heightened density may further alienate already stigmatized populations. Young men may find themselves more targeted for increased surveillance by police and security services. Moreover, many of the services located in low-income neighborhoods—welfare offices, food banks, second-hand stores—are no longer easily accessible as the socio-demographic character of the neighborhood changes leaving low-income individuals with increased

*Figure 2.4* The success of social mixing at Regent Park remains unclear as low-income populations are faced with a transformed urban community

Photo by Dan Zuberi

travel times or more expensive alternatives. Finally, a lack of social mixing means many of the anticipated lessons and benefits associated with 'model' middle-income neighbors have not been forthcoming. Instead, heightened animosity and alienation have decreased social capital and even reinforced racial and socioeconomic inequalities. According to Lees:

> Social mixing is being promoted through gentrification in the face of evidence that gentrification leads to social segregation, social polarization and displacement. The movement of middle-income groups to low-income areas creates overwhelmingly negative effects the most significant of which is the displacement of low-income groups. Far from being tolerant, gentrification is part of an aggressive, revanchist ideology designed to retake the inner city for the middle classes.
>
> (Lees 2008, 2457)

It is however important not to over-generalize or to unfairly romanticize low-income communities and the very real challenges faced by those living in poverty across North America. Frustration with housing quality and maintenance, concerns over safety, illicit activities and persistent stigmatization all remain problematic for many low-income residents (August 2014, 1320). However, networks of mutual assistance, respect for diversity, and a strong sense of belonging coexist with the types of grievances social redevelopment efforts attempted to address.

In this section, we have explored the predominant ethos behind public housing policy in both the United States and Canada and point to the emphasis on the strategy of social mix at the heart of most redevelopment efforts. We argue that despite considerable differences in both scale and national policy contexts between the two countries, the challenges faced by low-income populations—decreased social capital, alienation and stigmatization—share similarities. The promotion of social mix as a kind of self-help remedy to urban poverty ignores many of the ways in which inequality is reproduced socially and economically under conditions of neoliberalism. The emphasis on social mix and heavy reliance on private developers in redevelopment has reinforced what is in fact a 'false choice' between ongoing degradation of social housing infrastructure and gentrification at the heart of many contemporary urban redevelopment schemes.

## Urban Livability and Participatory Planning

If social mixing through urban renewal leaves low-income communities isolated and stigmatized, what alternative mechanisms exist to promote inclusive urban design? In the neoliberal era, individuals and cities are increasingly governed by the laws of the free market—competition, profit maximization, entrepreneurialism—while issues of social equity have largely disappeared from policy discourse. This is particularly disturbing given that income inequality and relative poverty in the United States are among the highest in the Organisation for Economic Co-operation and Development (OECD), having significantly increased over the last 40 years (Denk et al. 2013, 5). In Canada, too, the gap in income inequality has also grown substantially (Macdonald 2015). While pressure to pursue economic development remains pervasive across North American cities, critics increasingly point to widening social insecurity, uneven social-spatial development and the mounting socioeconomic failures of the neoliberal model of urban growth.

Combining principles of diversity, democracy and equity, Fainstein's (2010) theory of urban justice attempts move urban planning initiatives away from a solitary pursuit of economic development. Fainstein instead attempts to introduce normative criteria to move away from traditional political economy critiques and offer concrete alternative criteria and policies. She argues that justice, above all other considerations, should be the guiding principle of urban planning. Concretely, Fainstein argues that significant increases in affordable housing should be governed by a perpetuity in the affordable housing pool or be subject to one-to-one replacement; involuntary relocation of households or business should be ceased and voluntary movement adequately compensated; small business development should be given priority over large corporations; and mega-projects should be highly scrutinized and pursued only if direct benefits to low-income populations are realized (2010, 172–173).

While Fainstein (2010) admits that structural change is impossible on a municipal scale, she argues that changes in rhetoric and discourse can have profound effects on how socio-spatial inequality is managed. Fainstein's firmest point is that it is the equality of citizens in terms of fundamental rights—especially regarding the participation in public decision making—constitutes the starting point and ultimate objective of any just urban policy. In short, participatory planning practices must be more robustly realized. In the final section of this chapter, we explore how the City of Seattle, WA, has attempted to foster more inclusive community-driven decision making through the use of a comprehensive planning strategy that includes provisions for low-income housing. While many challenges remain, Seattle residents have been uniquely empowered to help shape the future development of their city.

## Participatory Planning in Seattle, WA

In the early 1990s, Washington State mandated that all urban municipalities were to prepare comprehensive plans for dealing with a high degree of projected population growth. The decision was the result of the Washington

State Legislature's Growth Management Act (GMA), passed in 1990, with the objective of reducing sprawl and curbing greenfield development state-wide. The legislation mandated that planning be undertaken to address: land use, transportation, housing, capital facilities and utilities. Over the next 5 years, the City of Seattle underwent an extensive neighborhood-planning

*Figure 2.5* The iconic Seattle Space Needle continues to define the city
Photo by Dan Zuberi

process. However, unlike other cities, Seattle not only elicited, but also financially supported, the contribution of thousands of Seattle residents. The result was the City of Seattle's Comprehensive Plan, the first comprehensive plan in the United States to explicitly target urban sustainability (Abdel et al. 2015, 15719).

*Figure 2.6* The innovative Experience Music Project Museum at Seattle Center, a $240-million celebration of music and its history

Photo by Dan Zuberi

The City of Seattle's Comprehensive Plan (1994–2014) was achieved through widespread public participation. The City provided residents with funding, guidance and guidelines to organize and make recommendations about the future of their communities. Undertaken over a 5-year period, it is estimated that over 20,000 people participated in the production of 38 neighborhood plans citywide. The result was a planning document explicitly created around a set of four 'core values': community, environmental stewardship, economic opportunity and security, and social equity. In 2007, the City Auditors' report found that 93 percent of the 800 people surveyed reported the planning and subsequent implementation processes to be positive (Blanco 2012, 194). The approach adopted by municipal planners in Seattle highlights how citizenship engagement can help to overcome many of the challenges associated top-down planning initiatives by fostering a sense of inclusiveness, empowerment and ownership over the future of a community. According to Blanco,

> Participation in a neighbourhood planning process is an indicator of an important social aspect of livability, the extent to which people who live and work in a neighbourhood have the ability to influence the characteristics and future development of their community. This is a primary democratic process.
>
> (Blanco 2012, 184)

The City has since renewed its vision for sustainability and commitment to public consultation through the development of Seattle 2035 Comprehensive Plan, the most recent attempt to address projected population growth of nearly 120,000 over the next 20 years (City of Seattle 2014). Yet, despite many of the achievements and innovative strategies undertaken by the city's planning authority, including an increase in low-income housing, wider pressures associated with gentrification and neoliberal restructuring are also apparent.

Between 1993 and 2013 approximately 60,000 new housing units were built across Seattle with the City funding upwards of 12,000 subsidized apartments for low-income individuals and families. In 2009, Seattle residents voted to renew a public housing levy and to provide an additional $145 million to preserve or produce 2,000 affordable housing units over the subsequent 7 years (City of Seattle 2014, 22). Moreover, the introduction of the Downtown Livability Legislation guaranteed affordable housing for city purchasers with incomes of up to 100 percent of the median income citywide (Riffkin 2009, 453–454). In the face of rising housing costs, including in those areas targeted for increased density, these efforts were an attempt to offset the pressures associated with rapid population growth and resulting gentrification.

There remain however important limitations to the comprehensive planning model adopted in Seattle in 1994 and which are still largely in effect today. Just as Fainstein (2010) noted in her Just City model for urban planning, strategies undertaken at the local level to curb the socioeconomic impacts of broader neoliberal restructuring are routinely subject to structural limitations. Between 2008 and 2012, nearly 13.2 percent of Seattle residents were living in poverty, while at the same time, the housing cost burden (measured by a percentage of households that spend 30 percent or more of their income on housing) ranged from 32 to 55 percent across Seattle's ten urban villages. The Seattle Sustainable Neighborhoods Assessment Project notes that despite the Comprehensive Plan's efforts to concentrate growth and employment in these areas, the outcome has not correlated higher densities with affordability (Steinbruek et al. 2014, 100–102). In 2006, the median home value in Seattle was 7.7 times greater than the median household income (Cohen 2007).

Critics argue that participatory planning and public consultation does not always protect or consider the needs of low-income residents. Purcell (2008) points to the Seattle neighborhood of South Lake Union as an example of how green revitalization and an ethos of environmental sustainability failed to address the needs to low-income residents. Dierwechter (2014) goes as far as to call the City's urban village model one of 'smart segregation', a nod to

*Figure 2.7* Construction cranes soar over Lake Union in Seattle
Photo by Dan Zuberi

the Whitening of Seattle's downtown core. In short, despite efforts to control growth and foster more participatory public engagement, many of the challenges of the neoliberal city remain. The recent introduction of a citywide mandatory minimum wage of $15 per hour by 2021 (compared to the federal rate of $7.25) is the latest attempt by policymakers to keep up with rising living costs and provide Seattle residents with a living wage. While political pressure to pursue equitable urban policies has been significant, wider trends associated with competitive city and neoliberal planning processes remain.

## Conclusion

In this chapter, we have explored the effects of neoliberal restructuring on access to and life in social housing in both Canada and the United States. We have attempted to reveal many of the underlying assumptions and objectives that drive the recent strategy of mixed-use and mixed-occupancy redevelopments. Without ignoring many of the real challenges faced by low-income communities living in depressed social housing facilities, including crime, insecurity and marginalization, we suggest that many of the perceived benefits associated with social mixing work to reinforce an individualized and pathological vision of poverty. The construction and management of housing continues to be

> at the forefront of attempts to regulate community relations and construct accepted norms of required behavior. Housing has, far more than any other pillars of the welfare state, such as education and health, been premised on conditionality of access linked to conduct, involving the moral classification of individuals as "deserving" and "undeserving".
>
> (Flint 2006, 7)

We argue that social housing must be a central component of any Just City alternative, but that it's governance must also include the participation of urban residents, most importantly those who are low income. The participatory model adopted in Seattle is perhaps an important first step in addressing the need for more equitable access to participation—both functionally and economically—but will always be subject to wider structural influences. Fostering the political will to combat the social and spatial consequences of neoliberal economic planning is fundamental.

## References

Abdel, T.D., White, J., and Clauson, S. (2015) "Risky Business: Sustainability and Industrial Land Use across Seattle's Gentrifying Riskscape", *Sustainability* 7(11): 15718–15753.

August, M. (2014) "Challenging the Rhetoric of Stigmatization: The Benefits of Concentrated Poverty in Toronto's Regent Park", *Environment and Planning*, 46: 1317–1333.

August M., and Walks, A. (2012) "From Social Mix to Political Marginalization? The Redevelopment of Toronto's Public Housing and the Dilution of Tenant Organizational Power", In G. Bridge, T. Butler, L. Lees, and T. Slater (eds.), *Mixed Communities: Gentrification by Stealth?* Bristol: The Policy Press. Pp. 273–298.

Axtell, R., and Tooley, M. (2015) "The Other Side of Hope: Squandering Social Capital in Louisville's HOPE VI", *Journal of Poverty*, 19(3): 278–304.

Bacher, J. (1993) *Keeping to the Marketplace: The Evolution of Canadian Housing Policy*. Montreal: McGill-Queens University Press.

Bauder, H. (2002) "Neighbourhood Effects and Cultural Exclusion", *Urban Studies*, 39(1), 85–93.

Birch, E.L. (2012) "Living Downtown in the Twenty-First Century: Past Trends and Future Policy Concerns", In F. Wagner and R. Caves (eds.), *Community Liveability: Issues and Approaches to Sustaining the Well-Being of People and Communities*. New York, NY: Routledge. Pp. 127–157.

Blanco, H. (2012) "Public Participation in Neighborhood Planning, a Neglected Aspect of Community Livability: The Case of Seattle", In F. Wagner and R. Caves (eds.), *Community Livability: Issues and Approaches to Sustaining the Well-Being of People and Communities*. New York, NY: Routledge. Pp. 183–197.

City of Seattle. (2014) "Seattle 2035 Updating Seattle's Comprehensive Plan: Backgrounder Report", www.seattle.gov/dpd/cs/groups/pan/@pan/documents/web_informational/p2112855.pdf [last accessed 19 July 2016].

Clark, W.A.V. (2008) "Reexamining the Moving to Opportunity Study and Its Contribution to Changing the Distribution of Poverty and Ethnic Concentration", *Demography*, 45(3), 515–535.

Cohen, A. "Home, Wage Gap Widens", *Seattle Post Intelligencer*. Published 11 September 2007. www.seattlepi.com/business/article/Home-wage-gap-widens-1249357.php [last accessed 20 July 2016].

DeFilippis, J. (2004) *Unmaking Goliath*. New York: Routledge.

DeFilippis, J., and Wyly, E. (2008) "Running to Stand Still: Through the Looking Glass with Federally-Subsidized Housing in New York City", *Urban Affairs Review*, 43(6): 777–816.

Denk, O., Hagemann, R.P., Lenain, P., and Somma, V. (2013) "Inequality and Poverty in the United States: Public Policies for Inclusive Growth", OECD Economics Department Working Papers, No. 1052, OECD Publishing. http://dx.doi.org/10.1787/5k46957cwv8q-en [last accessed 21 June 2016].

Dierwechter, Y. (2014) "The Spaces That Smart Growth Makes: Sustainability, Segregation, and Residential Change across Greater Seattle", *Urban Geography*, 35: 691–714.

Ellen, I.G., and Turner, M.A. (1997) "Does Neighbourhood Matter? Assessing Recent Evidence", *Housing Policy Debate*, 8(4): 833–866.

Fainstein, S. (2010) *The Just City*. Ithaca, NY: Cornell University Press.

Flint, J. (ed.). (2006) *Housing, Urban Governance and Anti-Social Behaviour: Perspectives, Policy, and Practice*. London, UK: The Policy Press.

Fraser, J.C., Burns, A.B., Bazuin, J.T., and Oakley, D.A. (2013) "HOPE VI, Colonization, and the Production of Difference", *Urban Affairs Review*, 49(4): 525–556.

Fraser, J.C., Oakley, D., and Bazuin, J. (2012) "Public Ownership and Private Profit in Housing", *Regions, Economy, and Society*, 5(3): 397–412.

Freeman, L. (2006) *There Goes the 'Hood: Views of Gentrification from the Ground Up*. Philadelphia, PA: Temple University Press.

Goetz, E.G. (2000) "The Politics of Poverty Deconcentration and Housing Demolition", *Urban Affairs*, 22(2): 157–173.

Goetz, E.G. (2003) *Clearing the Way: Deconcentrating the Poor in Urban America*. Washington, DC: Urban Institute Press.

Goetz, E.G. (2010) "Better Neighborhoods, Better Outcomes? Explaining Relocation Outcomes in HOPE VI", *Cityscape*, 12: 5–31.

Ireland, T.O., Thornberry, T.P., and Loeber, R. (2006) "Residential Stability among Adolescents in Public Housing: A Risk Factor for Delinquent and Violent Behaviour?" In J. Flint (ed.), *Housing, Urban Governance and Anti-Social Behaviour: Perspectives, Policy, and Practice*. London, UK: The Policy Press. Pp. 301–323.

James, R.K. (2010) "From 'Slum Clearance' to 'Revitalisation': Planning, Expertise and Moral Regulation in Toronto's Regent Park", *Planning Perspectives*, 25: 69–86.

Keels, M., Duncan, G.J., Deluca, S., Mendenhall, R., and Rosenbaum, J. (2005) "Fifteen Years Later: Can Residential Mobility Programs Provide a Long-Term Escape from Neighborhood Segregation, Crime, and Poverty?", *Demography*, 42(1): 51–73.

Keene, D.E., and Geronimus, A. (2011) "'Weathering' HOPE VI: The Importance of Evaluating the Population Health Impact of Public Housing Demolition and Displacement", *Urban Health*, 88(3): 417–435.

Kipfer, S., and Petrunia, J. (2009) "'Recolonization' and Public Housing: A Toronto Case Study", *Studies in Political Economy*, 83: 111–139.

Laakso, J. (2013) "Flawed Policy Assumptions and HOPE VI", *Journal of Poverty*, 17(1): 29–46.

Lees, L. (2014) "The Urban Injustices of New Labour's 'New Urban Renewal': The Case of the Aylesbury Estate in London", *Antipode*, 46(4): 921–947.

Lees, L. (2008) "Gentrification and Social Mixing: Towards an Inclusive Urban Renaissance?", *Urban Studies*, 45(12): 2449–2470.

Lens, M. (2014) "The Impact of Housing Vouchers on Crime in US Cities and Suburbs", *Urban Studies*, 51(6): 1274–1289.

Lipman, P. (2011) *The New Political Economy of Urban Education: Neoliberalism, Race, and the Right to the City*. New York, NY: Routledge.

Macdonald, D. (2015) "The Wealth Advantage: The Growing Wealth Gap between Canada's Affluent and Middle Classes", *The Canadian Centre for Policy Alternatives*. www.policyalternatives.ca/wealth-advantage [last accessed 20 September 2015].

Madanipour, A. (2010) "Introduction", In A. Madanipour (ed.), *Whose Public Space? International Case Studies in Urban Design and Development*. New York, NY: Routledge. Pp. 1–20.

Musterd, S., and Andersson, R. (2005) "Housing Mix, Social Mix and Social Opportunities", *Urban Affairs Review*, 40(6): 761–790.

Picton, R. (2010) "Selling National Urban Renewal: The National Film Board, the National Capital Commission, and Post-War Planning in Ottawa", *Urban History*, 37(2): 301–321.

Popkin, S.J., Rich, M.J., Hendey, L., Hayes, C., Parilla, J., and Glaster, G. (2012) "Public Housing Transformation and Crime: Making the Case for Responsible Relocation", *Cityscapes*, 14(3): 137–160.

Purcell, M. (2008) *Recapturing Democracy*. New York, NY: Routledge.

Purdy, S. (2003) "'Ripped Off' by the System: Housing Policy, Poverty, and Territorial Stigmatization in Regent Park Housing Project, 1951–1991", *Labour/Le Travail*, 52: 45–108.

Purdy, S. (2005) "Framing Regent Park: The National Film Board of Canada and the Construction of 'Outcast Spaces' in the Inner City, 1953 and 1994", *Culture and Society*, 27(4): 523–549.

Putnam, R. "Bowling Alone: America's Declining Social Capital", *Journal of Democracy*, 6(1): 65-87.

Riffkin, J.A. (2009) "Responsible Development? The Need for Revision to Seattle's Inclusionary Housing Plan", *Seattle University Law Review*, 32(2): 433–476.

Slater, T. (2006) "The Eviction of Critical Perspectives from Gentrification Research", *International Journal of Urban and Regional Research*, 30: 737–757.

Steinbrueck, P., Winter, M., Patterson, M., Williamson, S., Barbe, D., and Greaney, Y. (2014) "Seattle Sustainable Neighbourhoods Assessment Project", *SSNA Report 2014*. www.seattle.gov/dpd/cs/groups/pan/@pan/documents/web_informational/p2233677.pdf [last accessed 20 July 2016].

Thomas, J.M., and Hwang, H.H. (2003) "Social Equity in Redevelopment and Housing: The United States and Korea", *Journal of Planning Education and Research*, 23: 8–23.

Trudeau, D. (2006) "The Persistence of Segregation in Buffalo, New York: *Comer* vs. *Cisneros* and Geographies of Relocation Decisions among Low-Income Black Households", *Urban Geography*, 27(1): 20–44.

U.S. Department of Housing and Urban Development (HUD). (1974) *Statistical Yearbook*. Washington, DC: U.S. Government Printing Office (GPO).

Van Ham, M., Manley, D., Bailey, N., Simpson, L., and Maclennan, D. (2012) "Neighbourhood Effects Research: New Perspectives", In M. van Ham et al. (eds.), *Neighbourhood Effects Research: New Perspectives*. Springer: London. Pp. 1–21.

Verbeek, D.N. (2012) *Slum Clearance and Urban Renewal: A Demographic and Spatial Analysis of Changes in Downtown Halifax*. Halifax, NS: School of Planning, Dalhousie University.

Wade, J. (1994) *Houses for All: The Struggle for Social Housing in Vancouver 1919–1950*. Vancouver: UBC Press.

Wilson, J., and Kelling, G. (1982) "Broken Windows: The Police and Neighborhood Safety", *Atlantic Monthly*, 249(3): 29–38.

Wilson, W.J. (1987) *The Truly Disadvantaged: The Inner City, the Underclass and Public Policy*. Chicago, IL: University of Chicago Press.

Wilson, W.J. (1996) *When Work Disappears: The World of the New Urban Poor*. New York, NY: Vintage Books.

# 3 Creating New Urban Neighborhoods
## The Post-industrial Transformation From Brownfield to Vibrant Community?

Across North America, the legacy of industrialization can be found in the thousands of derelict or contaminated parcels of land scattered across urban communities. The product of intensive manufacturing during the late-nineteenth and early-twentieth centuries, recent shifts toward a more service-oriented economy—part and parcel of global economic restructuring—has left large swaths of urban real estate largely fallow, contaminated, and abandoned. Commonly referred to as brownfield land, the U.S. Environmental Protection Agency estimates that more than 450,000 brownfield sites currently exist in the United States (EPA 2015). Other sources put the number at well over 1 million sites (Greenberg et al. 2001).

In many large cities across North America, brownfields are the only readily available supply of land for new urban development, yet they remain commercially unviable because they are deemed too small or poorly located. Moreover, the financial liability associated with these sites' potential development long discouraged private investment. In this chapter, we explore recent attempts to develop brownfield land in a number of major North American metropolises. As governments have increasingly embraced strategies for sustainability and committed funds to promote environmental cleanup, many of the social-spatial inequalities associated with gentrification are routinely reproduced. As neoliberal urban planning embraces brownfield development as part and parcel of urban livability—and indeed sustainability—we ask how low-income populations are uniquely impacted. We find that while the threat of dislocation remains substantial, some communities have begun to demand a vision of sustainability that includes not only environmental, but also social considerations.

In the context of widespread suburbanization beginning in the 1960s, it made little financial sense to appropriate what was widely perceived as potentially hazardous urban land for alternative use. The term 'brownfield' distinguishes these former industrial sites from greenfield areas, under-developed suburban and rural lands on which real estate developers have historically preferred to build due to lower cost and lack of environmental contamination. However, as many North American cities have embraced a renewed process of urbanization, the sprawl associated with greenfield development is now largely understood as contributing to social, economic and environmental costs including poor air quality, gas consumption and ecological deterioration (Tang & Nathanail 2012; Eisen 2009).

As demand for revitalized and creative urban spaces continues to grow across North America, brownfield land now offers an attractive and potentially lucrative opportunity for development. This chapter explores trends in urban brownfield development across North America beginning in the mid-1980s. As a celebrated component of many Smart Growth urban initiatives, we argue that brownfield sites should be understood in the broader context of neoliberal urbanization and the gentrification of urban communities. Brownfield sites uniquely map the legacy of social-spatial dislocation across North American cities, epitomized by urban blight and the ghettoization of many established urban communities. As urban cores are increasingly subject to processes of gentrification, brownfield sites offer important spaces for debate around for who and what urban communities are made and remade in the context of some of North America's largest and most contaminated cities.

In the United States, federal law defines brownfield sites as "real property, the expansion, redevelopment, or reuse of which may be complicated by the presence or potential presence of hazardous substance, pollutant or contaminant" (EPA 2015). The term thus covers a wide array of both real and potentially contaminated sites including, but not limited to former waste disposal, manufacturing and service station facilities. Canada has largely adopted the American definition, though relative to the United States, the Canadian federal government has been less invested in these sites' redevelopment. In 1980, the U.S. Congress passed the Comprehensive Environmental Response, Compensation, and Liability Act (CERCLA), commonly referred to as the Superfund Act, which sought to cleanup brownfield sites by seeking financial accountability from those responsible for contamination. CERCLA also imposed heighted liability on developers engaged in brownfield projects. As a result, brownfields quickly became uncompetitive in the urban marketplace and were largely left idle.

Consequently many critics argue that while heightened liability rates do promote a degree of environmental protection, they also significantly raise the projected cost of contamination for businesses, discouraging investment and rendering brownfield sites largely uncompetitive in a free marketplace (Howland 2007, 92). From this perspective, the "draconian" measures demanded by CERCLA unnecessarily inhibit economic development, particularly in areas where contamination is minimal and cleanup relatively

*Figure 3.1* One of the oldest industrial areas of Toronto, Liberty Village, is today
among the city's most popular downtown neighborhoods

Photo by Dan Zuberi

straightforward (Meyer 2010, 55). In the context of deteriorating urban cores, CERCLA and its 1986 reauthorization, continues to be seen by some as contributing to the downfall of American cities by discouraging private investment.

In an effort to break down barriers to brownfield development in the United States, in 1997, the U.S. Congress authorized the Brownfields National Partnership Program, which earmarked $300 million to brownfield revitalization. In the years that followed over 5,000 sites were redeveloped largely through public–private partnerships, and in 2002, the Small Business Liability Relief and Brownfields Revitalization Act furthered funding for development. In 2009, coordination between the EPA, U.S. Department of Housing and Urban Development and the U.S. Department of Transportation resulted in the Partnership for Sustainable Communities, a program aimed at eliminating federal subsidies for projects that encourage urban sprawl. The same year, the American Recovery and Reinvestment Act provided the EPA's Brownfield Program with an additional $100 million in an effort to combat deteriorating housing markets brought on by recession. To date, the EPA has leveraged more than $6.5 billion in public and private funding for brownfield projects across the United States (Laitos & Abel 2011, 504–509).

The EPA now officially promotes brownfield development as part of its broader Smart Growth urban initiative, stressing that brownfield development shares "the same goals of providing economic growth, creating jobs, and creating a healthy environment" for U.S. communities (EPA 2015). An important goal of the EPA program is to create new jobs and sources of taxable revenue in urban areas by helping to attract new sources of private capital (Craighill et al. 2001, 515). While Canadian federal government officially endorses the development of brownfield land, to date, no federal subsidies exist to offset associated costs. With the exception of the province of Québec, in the Canadian context, significant provincial level funding is limited and no federal-level funding currently exists for brownfield development (De Sousa 2006, 395). Despite the lack of public funding or standardized guidelines for brownfield development in Canada, municipal governments are increasingly encouraging brownfield development through inventory projects and zoning reform. However, the cost associated with cleaning up brownfield sites remains a significant impediment to their redevelopment, particularly in the Canadian context where less public funding exists.

Despite consistencies between brownfield and Smart Growth development models, brownfields are distinct because of their fragmented and largely privatized orientation. In other words, while support for Smart Growth initiatives in both Canada and the United States are part of wider public sustainability planning, brownfields are developed on a parcel-by-parcel basis at the discretion of private investors (Eisen 2009, 10286–10287). Advocates of Smart Growth point to the potential of brownfield development for reducing public costs associated with new urban infrastructure projects, as well as the potential for environmental and aesthetic improvements (De Sousa 2002, 298). From this perspective, "the most significant costs to communities where underdeveloped brownfield sites are located come from the unrealized benefits of revitalization, and the opportunity costs of lands not yet changed into productive components of the local economy" (Laitos & Abel 2011, 499). In short, the uncertainty that stems from CERCLA's ongoing liability provisions produces a major disincentive for urban redevelopment (Slutzky & Frey 2010, 92); development that many policymakers see as imperative to wider revitalization and economic growth.

Policymakers and planners also routinely cite employment and higher quality housing as potentially under-tapped opportunities associated with brownfield development. However, while there are broad estimates of between 100,000 and 500,000 brownfield sites across the United States that are either underutilized or abandoned (Craighill et al. 2001, 515), empirical data on their characteristics are limited (Wernstedt & Hanson 2009, 135). In Canada, as much as 25 percent of urban areas are estimated to be potentially contaminated based on past industrial uses, and national-level estimates range broadly from 2,999 to 30,000 (De Sousa 2006, 394). In both countries, no systematic national-level brownfield studies currently exist, which admittedly limits our understanding of their contribution to wider socio-spatial trends. Yet, preliminary evidence suggests that when considered as part of broader processes of urban revitalization, brownfield development as currently practiced may exacerbate existing socio-spatial trends (Tang & Nathanail 2012; Greenberg & Lewis 2000; Porter 2009).

Critics of current brownfield development initiatives point to local-area impacts of what is a largely piecemeal and market-oriented approach to development. Eisen notes that in the context of the United States, states do not generally require that brownfield projects fit in to community-level planning and that no long-term evaluation mechanisms are currently in place (2009, 10287). In other words, little attention is currently paid to how brownfield redevelopment projects contribute to (or disrupt) existing community planning. In Canada, the Brownfields Statute Law Amendment Act came into effect in 2004 in the province of Ontario, removing some of financial barriers associated with brownfield cleanup and providing more legal protection to investors, thus enhancing the confidence and predictability of developing brownfield sites. However, to date, no regional- or community-level regulations exist governing brownfield land use. For McCarthy, this

*Figure 3.2* The old is made new again as former industrial sites are reimaged for commercial and residential use

Photo by Dan Zuberi

is problematic because brownfields disproportionately impact low-income, racialized or otherwise disenfranchised communities, and therefore pose serious challenges for the achievement of spatial and social equity (2009, 226). In the context of the neoliberal city, the exploitation of brownfields for primarily their economic and aesthetic potential raises important questions about how brownfields contribute to wider processes of gentrification and social inequity.

Yet, proponents, including many city mayors and members of U.S Congress, continue to celebrate brownfield development as untapped sources of job creation, particularly in areas where unemployment and poverty have been longstanding issues. However, studies vary considerably in their estimations of brownfield contribution to employment. Optimistic estimates suggest that as many as 236,000 jobs could be created across more than one hundred U.S. cities, generating up to half a billion dollars in tax revenue (Greenberg & Lewis 2000, 2512). The U.S. Conference of Mayors in 2000 estimated that brownfields could produce over 550,000 jobs and $2.4 billion in additional tax revenue. Finally, the EPA reports that its Brownfield Program has created in the range of 25,000 new jobs across the United States (Laitos & Abel 2011, 509). Despite these widely disparate claims, it remains the case that because central cities are no longer magnets for manufacturing, many brownfield sites are being redeveloped for commercial and residential, rather than industrial uses. This in turn raises questions about the type and quality of any jobs that are in fact created through brownfield revitalization. For example, Howland notes there is little evidence to suggest that jobs created from brownfield development are permanent, full-time or go to those who were previously un- or underemployed (Howland 2007, 93). As the private sector approaches brownfield development as opportunities to profit from large and under-exploited patches of real estate, they tend to be developed in or adjacent to areas already seen as attractive and competitive for investment. While employment may be a positive effect of brownfield redevelopment, questions over who occupies these positions and their overall quality are compounded by the gentrifying influence of their market-driven locale.

Studies show that larger brownfield sites, located in attractive urban areas, such as central business districts, subway lines, waterfronts or major retail areas, can be economically viable for developers, despite high costs associated with land cleanup and remediation (Meyer & Lyons 2000; Pepper 1997; McCarthy 2002, 293). In other words, even with heightened liability on brownfield sites, developers are keen to capitalize on growing demand for urban amenities, particularly those that promote creative and livable urban communities. For example, De Sousa (2002) finds that in the case of Toronto, Canada city councilors successfully fostered an 'urban image' in

*Figure 3.3* Condos in Toronto's Liberty Village are routinely priced beyond the
        financial means of most middle- and low-income populations
Photo by Dan Zuberi

order to lure both people and capital back into depressed areas, contributing in turn to the investment potential of brownfield projects (De Sousa
2002, 306). Yet while small businesses and lower-income residents may
benefit indirectly from brownfield development, the concentrated nature of
projects in economically ripened geographic areas means that gentrification pressures can push out lower-income populations. Moreover, according
to Wernstedt and Hanson the opportunistic site-by-site redevelopment of
brownfield land parcels tends to perpetuate more homogenous neighborhoods. They note, "[S]uccessful progressive development by definition will
bring increased property prices and rents, promoting gentrification that may
push out long time residents and dilute the number of local business owners
in the area" (2009, 141).

Despite the potential for job creation and increased tax revenues associated with brownfield development, limited empirical evidence supports
the sociological benefits of brownfield development (Howland 2007, 95).
Although brownfield land, and particularly those sites with high degrees of
contamination, tend to be located in and around economically depressed
urban areas, cleanup does not necessarily restore inclusive or equitable
urban communities.

While gentrification may make physical improvements aimed at promoting the livability of previously depressed areas, the displacement of former residents can exacerbate socio-spatial inequalities by concentrating poverty elsewhere (Tang & Nathanail 2012, 843), often in peripheral areas largely cut off from urban centers. Because developers are able to target contaminated, but otherwise marketable sites for redevelopment, many of the most hazardous sites remain untouched thus disproportionately impacting already geographically isolated communities (McCarthy 2002, 293). A review of the disparate literature on brownfield development reveals that a recurrent challenge for policymakers is the concentration of sites in highly distressed urban communities, raising questions about the opportunity cost of redevelopment in areas deemed unattractive by the market.

Even in the United States where public subsidies exist to help offset the cost of cleanup, disproportionately high rates of deteriorating infrastructure, poverty and low-skilled workers make many of these more isolated brownfield sites uncompetitive for development. For example, McCarthy (2009) finds that in the case of Milwaukee brownfield redevelopments between 1990 and 2005 were disproportionately concentrated in nonminority census track areas, despite the fact that the vast majority of the city's brownfield land is situated in minority and low-income areas. In another case example, Baltimore's American Can Co. project was chosen strategically for its waterfront location and minimal cleanup requirements, and the development has resulted in a high-end condominium community (Howland 2007, 97).

In the United States, meeting the housing needs of urban communities has never been an explicit goal of the EPA brownfield remediation program (Greenberg et al. 2001, 515). Increasing local tax bases and fostering employment opportunities remain central to public financing of brownfield areas. However, as previously outlined, housing shortages—particularly of affordable housing—remains a significant problem across both U.S. and Canadian cities. This has led some to suggest that brownfield sites could and indeed should be developed to help to provide quality and affordable housing in increasingly populated urban areas (Greenberg 2002; Greenberg et al. 2001; McCarthy 2002, 2009; Meyer 2010). Advocates argue that demographic projections make residential development highly attractive to urban developers who, despite higher cleanup costs, could reap considerable returns in the residential marketplace. Others counter these claims by arguing that high rates of residential development will, in the long run, adversely impact urban restructuring by diminishing employment in the urban core. In other words, while affordable housing remains an important component of urban planning, condos do not create long-term employment, and their affordability is far from guaranteed.

## Cleaning Up Across North America

The City of Toronto has experienced a 'redevelopment miniboom' of residential brownfield revitalization since the early 1990s. In the face of declining manufacturing into the 1980s, the City used zoning bylaws to accommodate more diverse uses of urban real estate. Between 1988 and 1998, 80 percent of Toronto's industrial sites were re-zoned for alternative activities (Hemson 1998). In total, approximately 424 acres of former industrial land, primarily in the downtown core was directly impacted (De Sousa 2002, 299). Among the largest brownfield development sites in the city's history, Liberty Village is a 45-acre site on the western edge of Toronto's downtown. A former manufacturing district, in 2001 the City officially designated Liberty Village a Business Improvement Area in an effort to attract new creative and high-tech industries. Today, Liberty Village is one of the fastest growing business hubs in the city with commercial and residential property values now well in excess of national averages. And while many business leaders and municipal planners celebrate the success of Liberty Village as a model of urban sustainability and mix-use planning, the area's former working-class residents have been largely outpriced of their community (Catungal 2009).

Across many Canadian cities, residential brownfield redevelopment reflects the strong residential marketplace in major cities, and the tendency of policymakers to capitalize on rising housing prices. In fact, De Sousa finds Toronto to be emblematic of a wider trend across 12 Canadian cities in that 47 percent of remediation projects have been residential, compared to 20 percent retail, 16 percent commercial, 12 percent open spaced, and just 2 percent industrial and institutional respectively. In Toronto, residential projects took place throughout the central city, concentrating in the central business and entertainment districts in the southwest and southeast (De Sousa 2002, 302). The King-Spadina area just west of the city's business district offers a particularly strong example of the prototypical 'hip' and creative image Toronto has successful marketed and the shifting demographic trends of residents who can afford to live there. As outlined in previous chapters, pressures associated with rising real estate and gentrified communities in Toronto has served to exacerbate social-spatial inequalities by pushing out lower-income residents, who are increasingly residing in inner-ring suburbs and other suburban communities.

While advocates of brownfield redevelopment routinely cite demand for urban housing, even in cases where significant growth has occurred, concerns remain around its access and affordability. As Rubinstein has noted, even when mixed-use and affordable housing are deemed the best use of brownfield land, the reality remains that affordable housing is not rewarded in a competitive urban marketplace. "Given that affordable housing rarely if

*Figure 3.4* A crane works to complete a number of new residential towers
Photo by Dan Zuberi

ever generates a commercial market equivalent rate of return, these increased environmental development costs associated with affordable housing [on brownfield land] complicate financing and development" (Rubinstein 2004, 364). And while residential use remains the dominant trend across Canadian cities, no federal funding currently exists to promote offset high costs and promote non-market pricing.

In contrast, in the United States, a depressed residential housing market and the infusion of federal funds for brownfield redevelopment has largely promoted commercial as opposed to residential activity. In both cases, brownfield revitalization has significantly altered urban environments and raised important questions about the socioeconomic homogenization of urban communities. Yet, while these general trends remain concerning, some alternative strategies are also beginning to emerge.

While funding and implementation of piecemeal brownfield revitalization remains challenging in both Canada and the United States, more inclusive and area-wide approaches to development are also evident. Community Land Trusts and progressive financing models are providing alternatives to market mechanism and are in turn better able to support social and community needs. Affording communities "the means of exercising voice, a stake in remediation and regeneration, and capacity for monitoring and protecting themselves over time" remain important goals of alternative development strategies (Meyer 2010, 63).

Critics of currently parcel-by-parcel brownfield development have long argued that states should do more to integrate brownfield remediation into larger sustainable and regional planning (Eisen 2009; McCarthy 2002, 2009; Green 2000). Increasingly cities in New York and New Jersey have established area-wide brownfield initiatives in an effort to address multiple brownfield sites located in the same larger community (Eisen 2009, 10288). However, many developers and even some public officials continue to view community consultation as a time consuming and expensive impediment to brownfield development, despite evidence suggesting that community input helps encourage consensus-building and may prevent future protests and litigation (McCarthy 2002, 249).

Scholars are increasingly highlighting growing demand for the consideration of social impacts in brownfield revitalization projects (Armstrong & Verma 2005; Timney 1998; McCarthy 2009). Indeed as Aguesloviski (2015) argues, the environmental discourse surrounding efforts to promote brownfield cleanup too often neglects the sociological components of sustainability. In other words, there is great potential for inequality, privilege, gentrification and social-spatial dislocation to be reinforced when brownfields are developed with aesthetic and economic as opposed to social justice considerations.

In the United States Greenpoint, Brooklyn provides an important example of successful community integration into brownfield planning. Located in the northernmost part of Brooklyn and bordered by Newton Creek and the East River, Greenpoint was once an important hub of industrial and marine activity. Shipbuilding, printing, glass blowing, iron production and the refining of petroleum together over time contributed to substantial contamination of the surrounding environment. Historically home to predominantly Irish and Italian working-class families, today the neighborhood also boasts large Polish and Latino immigrant and working-class communities. According to Curran and Hamilton,

> The greening of Greenpoint has taken many forms, from the recent declaration of Newtown Creek as a Superfund site, to historical battles against a waste incinerator and a new power plant, to more superficial interventions such as the construction of a local nature trail. In each case, local, long-term activists have been at the forefront of these environmental battles and crucial to the construction of an environmental vision that both greens the neighborhood while also maintaining its working-class character and allowing room for community residents to participate in the process. These processes, . . . have . . . allowed for

alternative visions of economic development, social justice, and resource use.

(Curran and Hamilton 2012, 1033)

These authors argue that successful challenge to further gentrification in Greenpoint has been the result of strategic alliances among local activists and the insistence that any definition of sustainability must also include attention to social justice. The development of a common set of norms and values amongst city planners, developers and community members has been key to the area's redevelopment (Hamilton & Curran 2012). In this way, gentrification has not led to the eradication of the area's industrial legacy or its working-class heritage and any social-spatial dislocation brought on my its development have been limited.

Indeed, the case of Greenpoint, Brooklyn where community members successfully contested practices of environmental gentrification, offers a potentially powerful counter-example to the dominant trend. Curran and Hamilton (2012) show how "[d]ecades of environmental activism by long-term residents and collaboration with more recent in-movers, many of whom are gentrifiers, has resulted in a cleanup process that actively contests the assumed outcome of environmental gentrification" (1028). By rejecting a sustainability strategy that did not include industrial use or blue-collar workers, residents of Greenpoint insisted on a definition of sustainable renewal that incorporated existing lower-income communities. In other words, the 'greening' of Greenpoint was achieved without the disappearance of working-class families. A strategy of 'just green enough' demanded an important balance between environmental and social justice concerns.

Similarly, Lee and Mohai (2013) find that in the rust belt of the American Northeast, Detroit, Michigan, has made important steps toward the regeneration of brownfield land. They argue that unlike other U.S. cities where brownfield land adjacent to desirable real estate is prioritized for cleanup in Detroit disadvantaged areas have been uniquely targeted. The area known as Detroit/Wayne County currently includes more than 3,000 brownfield sites, including more than 1,800 that are directly contaminating the Detroit River. These sites are overwhelmingly located in communities with the highest concentration of racial minorities and lowest levels of income (EPA 2010). Established in 1996, the Detroit Brownfield Redevelopment Authority has since pursued cleanups of over 198 brownfield sites at a cost of well over $5 billion USD. According to the Detroit Economic Growth Corporation, these projects have included residential, mixed-use, retail, office and commercial uses, which together are expected to contribute 18,500 new jobs and 10,000 new housing units across the city (DEGC 2016). Areas including Midtown and New Center have been particularly impacted with many abandoned and former industrial sites being transformed for residential and commercial use (Jackson 2009, 324). Yet, while scholars note that revitalization of distressed urban areas such as those in Detroit is an important component of the EPA's attention to environmental justice, many fail to consider how low-income populations are perversely impacted after development occurs. Indeed, Detroit offers an important example of brownfield redevelopment in an area with higher concentration of minorities and low-income populations. Lee and Mohai (2011) find that brownfield neighborhoods in Detroit are made up of 58.2 percent African-American residents; by contrast, non-brownfield sites house a mere 20.7 percent. Brownfield neighborhoods in Detroit are also poorer with 21.1 percent of households living below the U.S. poverty line. While the Detroit Brownfield Redevelopment Authority explicitly aims to improve the economic conditions of brownfield areas, projects are largely determined by a site's potential for redevelopment, often understood in economic rather than social terms. It remains the case that in much of the United States and Canada, brownfield redevelopment continues to overwhelmingly respond almost exclusively to market, as opposed to social conditions and is routinely pursued on a site-by-site basis, leaving little room for broader public consultation or social-spatial considerations.

A brownfield development strategy that privileges private developers and that is dictated by market forces is largely unaccountable to broader public interests such as long-term affordable housing and quality employment. While brownfields tend to be concentrated in urban areas across North America, they also disproportionately impact low-income and minority populations, populations already adversely impacted by broader economic change. As neoliberal global economic restructuring continues to drive urbanization, many cities are seeing high skilled creative, technological and service industries replace manufacturing and transform cities. Overall brownfield redevelopment patterns reflect the broader pattern of the devaluation of social justice, participatory engagement and the interests of low-income residents.

## Conclusion

Brownfields offer important sites of revitalization, but are also uniquely subject to the pressures of gentrification. As demand for livable, creative and consumer-driven urban neighborhoods continue to shape municipal planning, the interests of vulnerable populations are often ignored or devalued. While governments must work to attract investment in contaminated brownfield areas, they should also ensure that land use remains connected to broader community needs. Integrating meaningful community participation and even ownership into urban brownfield development strategies may help to mitigate harm, but without government oversight and intervention, brownfield redevelopment will continue to respond primarily to the interests of developers and the wealthy, which will shape the social-spatial inequalities of cities in the future.

The brownfield projects with the greatest financial feasibility tend to be those already well suited for gentrification. As brownfield sites are developed in an open marketplace, those with the highest potential for maximum profit generation are targeted for cleaned up, often with limited consideration of pre-existing social realities or conditions. Indeed, the most hazardous and highly concentrated site areas are disproportionately located in low-income and minority urban neighborhoods. As a result, the brownfield sites that are developed respond to market demands for more high-quality and livable urban communities, can create the conditions that result in the eviction and outmigration of lower-income residents. These residents in turn add to existing pressures in other low-income communities where brownfield development in least likely to occur and where disproportionate health impacts, including cancer and respiratory disease, are also well documented (McCarthy 2009, 215; Timney 1998; Litt et al. 2002). While urban employment statistics and taxable revenues are potentially increased with brownfield development, there is little evidence to suggest that the benefits of current brownfield redevelopment projects are distributed equitably or help to reduce socio-spatial dislocation. In the United States, public support for brownfield cleanup has tended to support commercial as opposed to residential projects (Howland 2007, 99), which has been linked to employment growth. However, in Canada, in the absence of public financing, brownfield projects have responded to heightened demand for residential as opposed to commercial or industrial property uses. While demand for increased residential urban spaces continues to grow, condos only create limited employment. While the cleanup of environmentally hazardous sites is both desirable and necessary, it should not be pursued without consideration of the sociological dimensions of sustainability. Without attention to social and spatial dimensions of inequality, brownfield redevelopment under conditions of neoliberalism can in fact exacerbate processes of gentrification and exclusion.

## References

Aguesloviski, I. (2015) "From Toxic Sites to Parks as (Green) LULUs? New Challenges of Inequity, Privilege, Gentrification, and Exclusion for Urban Environmental Justice", *Journal of Planning Literature*, 31:1–14.

Armstrong, C.S., and Verma, N. (2005) "The Social Construction of Brownfields", The Association of European Schools of Planning Conference, Vienna, Austria. http://citeseerx.ist.psu.edu/viewdoc/download;jsessionid=C0090A4D654963D0 B825424EBCB9C1FF?doi=10.1.1.540.7181&rep=rep1&type=pdf [last accessed 22 December 2015].

Catungal, J.P. (2009) "Geographies of Displacement in the Creative City: The Case of Liberty Village, Toronto", *Urban Studies*, 46(5–6): 1095–1114.

Craighill, P., Wells, J., and Greenberg, M. (2001) "Brownfield Redevelopment and Affordable Housing: A Case Study of New Jersey", *Housing Policy Debate*, 12(3): 515–540.

Curran, W., and Hamilton, T. (2012) "Just Green Enough: Contesting Environmental Gentrification in Greenpoint, Brooklyn", *Local Environment*, 17: 1027–1042.

De Sousa, C. (2002) "Brownfield Redevelopment in Toronto: An Examination of Past Trends and Future Prospects", *Land Use Policy*, 19(4): 297–309.

De Sousa, C. (2006) "Urban Brownfields Redevelopment in Canada: The Role of Local Government", *Canadian Geographer*, 50(3): 392–407.

Detroit Economic Growth Commission. "Detroit Brownfield Redevelopment Authority". www.degc.org/about-degc/detroit-brownfield-redevelopment-authority-1 [last accessed 16 August 2016].

Eisen, J.B. (2009) "Brownfields Development: From Individual Sites to Smart Growth", *Environmental Law Reporter: News and Analysis*, 39(4): 10285–10290.

Environmental Protection Agency (EPA). (2010) "Brownfields 2010 Revolving Loan Fund Grant Fact Sheet: Detroit/Wayne Country Port Authority, MI", *EPA Brownfields Program*. https://cfpub.epa.gov/bf_factsheets/gfs/index.cfm?xpg_id=7245&display_type=HTML [last accessed 16 August 2016].

Environmental Protection Agency (EPA). (2015) "Brownfield Overview and Definition", *U.S. Environmental Protection Agency*. www.epa.gov/brownfields/brownfield-overview-and-definition [last accessed 23 December 2015].

Green, N.L. (2000) *Promoting More Equitable Brownfield Redevelopment*. Cambridge, MA: Lincoln Institute of Land Policy.

Greenberg, M. (2002) "Should Housing Be Built on Former Brownfield Sites?", *American Journal of Public Health*, 92(5): 703–705.

Greenberg, M., Craighill, H.P., Mayer, C.Z., and Wells, J. (2001) "Brownfield Redevelopment and Affordable Housing: A Case Study of New Jersey", *Housing Policy Debate*, 12(3): 515–540.

Greenberg, M., and Lewis, J.M. (2000) "Brownfields Redevelopment, Preferences and Public Involvement: A Case Study of an Ethnically Mixed Neighbourhood", *Urban Studies*, 37(13): 2501–2514.

Hamilton, T., and Curran, W. (2012) "From Five Angry Women to Kick-Ass Community: Gentrification and Environmental Activism in Brooklyn and Beyond", *Urban Studies*, 50(8): 1557–1574.

Hemson. (1998) *Retaining Employment Lands: Morningside Heights: A Report to the City of Toronto Economic Development, Tourism and Culture*. Toronto: Hemson Consulting.

Howland, M. (2007) "Employment Effects of Brownfield Redevelopment: What Do We Know from the Literature?", *Journal of Planning Literature*, 22(2): 91–107.

Jackson, G.W., Jr. (2009) "Bridging Two Communities in Detroit: A Brownfield Connection", *Environmental Practice*, 11(4): 324–327.

Laitos, J.G., and Abel, T.H. (2011) "The Role of Brownfields as Sites for Mixed Use Development Projects in America and Britain", *Denver Journal of International Law and Policy*, 40(1–3): 492–514.

Lee, S., and Mohai, P. (2011) "Racial and Socioeconomic Assessment of Neighborhoods Adjacent to Small-Scale Brownfield Sites in the Detroit Region", *Environmental Practice*, 13: 340–353.

Lee, S., and Mohai, P. (2013) "The Socioeconomic Dimensions of Brownfield Cleanup in the Detroit Region", *Population and Environment*, 34(3): 420–429.

Litt, J., Tran, N., and Burke, T. (2002) "Examining Urban Brownfields through the Public Health 'Macroscope'", *Environmental Health Perspectives*, 110: 183–193.

McCarthy, L. (2002) "The Brownfield Dual Land-Use Policy Challenge: Reducing Barriers to Private Redevelopment while Connecting Reuse to Broader Community Goals", *Land Use Policy*, 19: 287–296.

McCarthy, L. (2009) "Off the Mark? Efficiency in Targeting the Most Marketable Sites Rather Than Equity in Public Assistance for Brownfield Redevelopment", *Economic Development Quarterly*, 23(3): 211–228.

Meyer, P.B. (2010) "Brownfields, Risk-Based Corrective Action, and Local Communities", *Cityscape*, 12(3): 55–69.

Meyer, P.B., and Lyons, T. (2000) "Lessons from Private Sector Brownfield Redevelopers", *Journal of the American Planning Association*, 66: 46–57.

Pepper, E. (1997) *Lessons from the Field: Unlocking Economic Potential with an Environmental Key*. Washington, DC: Northeast-Midwest Institute.

Porter, M. (2009) "The Geography of New York State's Brownfield Cleanup Program: Population and Land Value Characteristics of Areas Surrounding New York City Properties Enrolled in New York State's Brownfield Cleanup Program", *Environmental Practice*, 11(4): 245–255.

Rubinstein, R.D. (2004) "Developing Affordable Housing on Brownfields: Implementing the 'Joseph Paradigm'", *Journal of Affordable Housing & Community Development Law*, 13(3): 364–383.

Slutzky, D., and Frey, A.J. (2010) "Brownfields Uncertainty: A Proposal to Reform Superfund", *Cityscape*, 12(3): 85–100.

Tang, Y.T., and Nathanail, P.C. (2012) "Sticks and Stones: The Impact of the Definitions of Brownfield in Policies on Socio-Economic Sustainability", *Sustainability*, 4(12): 840–862.

Timney, M. (1998) "Environmental Injustices", In D. Camacho (ed.), *Environmental Injustices, Political Struggles*. Durham, NC: Duke University Press. Pp. 179–193.

Wernstedt, K., and Hanson, J. (2009) "Community Revitalization through Areawide Brownfield Regeneration, Community Land Trusts, and Progressive Finance", *Environmental Practice*, 11(3): 134–143.

# 4 Urban Renewal in Vancouver, Canada

Ranked the most livable city in the world for eight consecutive years between 2002 and 2010, Vancouver, Canada, has garnered international recognition for the quality of life afforded to its 2.3 million residents. As Canada's third largest city, Vancouver's population growth in 2011 was second only to the country's largest city, Toronto, and the metropolitan region is home to over 50 percent of the population of the province of British Columbia (Metro Vancouver 2012). Population demands continue to drive urban infrastructure development and substantial investments in mega-projects, including those associated with the 2010 Winter Olympics, have helped promote the appeal of urban living, particularly among younger demographics. As more and more young professionals seek to make Vancouver home, changes to the economic and social fabric of the city are being challenged in ways that both reinforce existing divisions and create new opportunities for community, sustainability and commerce.

Broader trends in neoliberal economic and political reorganization have been highly pervasive in North American cities since the decline of the manufacturing era. The revitalization of once industrialized downtown cores helped spark a return to urban living as a desirable, affordable and practical choice for modern young professionals. Whether individual city planning or larger social and cultural shifts have precipitated this change, the renewal of urban centers and the creation of urban communities have been facilitated by gentrification practices advanced by local governments and financed in large part by public–private partnerships and foreign investments. In Vancouver, this trend has sparked debate over the political agendas of city officials, the dramatic rise in the cost of living and soaring real estate prices, and who and what are to be included in the maintenance and development of new urban communities. While questions of access and rights to the city continue to be part of the dialogue, the solutions are now decidedly more balanced toward public–private partnerships and other market-oriented approaches. For example, community centers and public parks have become private sector concessions granted in exchange for the right to exceed height restrictions and maximize profits. How urban livability is framed is of central importance to the maintenance of this shifting trend in urban development.

Gentrification, or urban renewal, has occurred in Vancouver in varying degrees across the metropolitan area over the preceding decades; however, particular neighborhoods have been uniquely targeted including Yaletown, Granville Island, False Creek and Gastown. Though developed independently, each neighborhood is representative of larger social, political and economic trends employed by urban scholars to make intelligible these material transformations. Conceptualized as manifestations of neoliberal urban renewal (Brenner & Theodore 2003), contemporary gentrification practices transform urban landscapes and challenge planners to expand definitions of revitalization beyond economic measures of property value and income demographics (Bright 2000). Growing concerns about the social and economic impacts of urban communities have ignited discussion of, and resistance to, the monopolization of urban space by privileged groups and the systematic exclusion of disadvantaged communities, many of whom have long occupied contemporary sites of urban gentrification practices.

*Figure 4.1* Cranes tower over rising condo high-rise buildings in Southeast False Creek, Vancouver

Photo by Dan Zuberi

A process of decentralization typifies the Canadian experience of urban gentrification and, particularly in Vancouver, this has meant an increasing proportion of land use dedicated to residential purposes (especially condominium towers), largely driven by an influx of university-educated young adult populations. This new 'creative class' of entrepreneurs, technological innovators and young professionals have been held responsible for indirectly spurring a dramatic increase in population density in Vancouver's downtown core, which has simultaneously resulted in substantial reductions in average residential square footage as well as low-income properties over the last two decades (Florida 2003; Boyle & Haggerty 2011). A flood of middle-and upper-middle class professionals to North American urban centers, like Vancouver, has significantly increased the demand for residential properties and created a high-value housing market that some argue increasingly excludes the interests of lower-income individuals and families (Allen 2008). Moreover, the emphasis on residential development has come at the cost of office space and other commercial uses of land in the city.

Vancouver's changing population has spawned what scholars refer to as a 'new economy', which is seen by some as the driving force behind the urban renewal of the city's downtown core, particularly in the highly gentrified neighborhoods of Yaletown and Gastown. Increasingly these neighborhoods are home to young, well-paid professionals working in technological and creative fields of design and communication (Boyle & Haggerty 2011; Hutton 2004a; Danyluk & Ley 2007). Danyluk and Ley (2007) find increasingly liberal, anti-suburbia ideologies to be associated with Vancouver's downtown gentrified communities. This sentiment is echoed by Ley (1997) in his assessment of the distinctive culture of a new class of urban professionals. Rejecting the bourgeois and unsustainable legacy of North American suburbanization, the 'new middle class' are among the most privileged members of contemporary urban society, and are arguably the strongest driving force behind renewed gentrification processes.

As the North American economy shifts decidedly away from manufacturing to the service sector, these urban newcomers have become an integral part of the transformation and regeneration of formally disused industrial and/or disenfranchised urban areas into thriving metropolitan centers of commerce. Yet their success comes at a cost to the affordability and accessibility of many traditional urban populations, including newcomer immigrants and refugees who are increasingly bypassing urban centers in favor of more affordable edge cities and suburban communities.

Cities provide important sites of economic growth, cultural production and consumption practices for a metropolitan region. Yet the notably undemocratic, exclusionary production of new spaces has been repeatedly invoked as the driving force behind urban unrest and volatility through direct and indirect displacement of vulnerable populations (Rerat et al. 2010; Pollard 2004). The June 2011 Stanley Cup riot, which erupted with the loss of the National Hockey League Championship game to Boston, besieged the city and captured the attention of the world, may reflect simmering submerged tensions and unrest reflective of the neoliberal era, even in a region known as Lotusland and home of Lululemon yoga wear. Vancouver may be just one example among many of shifting demographic and cultural cityscapes; however, it is also a unique illustration of the potential for renewal projects to contribute to sustainable, livable and more inclusive North American cities.

## Urban Redevelopment: Vancouver, Canada

New and emerging industries have helped transform Vancouver from its resource, manufacturing and port-centered origins to its current position as a global leader in technological and creative innovation. The volatile nature of these new industries stands in sharp contrast to the relative stability of the manufacturing era, and poses new and recurring challenges for municipal policymakers and planners. The globalized nature of Vancouver's domestic employment market further upsets traditional notions of work and place as modern infrastructure projects struggle to adapt to the changing needs and demands of its population. Moreover, the 'new economy' in Vancouver is, according to Barnes and Hutton (2009), uniquely characterized by the geographical context and the particular trajectory of the city itself. Bounded by waterfront and mountain terrain, Vancouver has long avoided the sprawl associated with most other North American cities. Punter (2003) has argued that geography, in part, has helped to shape municipal planning in Vancouver into a world-renowned leader in urban regeneration and development. An innovative approach to mega-project planning, discretionary zoning practices and strategic neighborhood-planning practices have also helped to market the desirability of Vancouver as a city in which to live and invest.

The modern North American city is marked by creative innovation and an interdependence between production and consumption in marked clusters of development. The young professional living, working and playing in the city's downtown core is both a new and emerging model of urban life in Vancouver and one that produces layered and interconnected sociopolitical, spatial, and economic challenges. Regeneration is associated with a persistent trend of dislocation and even conflict. Gentrification often results in decreases in economic and ethnic diversity within urban communities, as well as inter-neighborhood isolation and inequality. Keeping gentrified neighborhoods socially and economically diverse, scholars argue, remains key to curbing unrest (Squires 1989; Walks & Maaranen 2008).

*Figure 4.2*  The Vancouver Art Gallery with adjacent Fairmont hotel and luxury residential tower

Photo by Dan Zuberi

Though the City of Vancouver has largely succeeding in meeting the distinctive interests of the public according to some, processes of gentrification and urban renewal have simultaneously created new social conflicts, tensions and displacements for Vancouver's most vulnerable populations (Hutton 2004a, 2008).

Meligrana and Skaburskis (2005) point out that Vancouver is the only gentrified Canadian city to increase both population *and* density, largely due to its unique geographic boundaries. The demand for rental properties has fueled a nearly two-fold increase in the number of non-family households in the city's downtown core leaving some to point exclusively to population movements as the driving force behind the dislocation of some vulnerable residents of these booming neighborhoods (Hutton 2004a, 2008; Ley 1994, 1997). However, Davidson and Lees (2010) argue that demographic transformations, and the urban development it appears to stimulate, are relatively innocuous. They consider the process of urban displacement to be far more nuanced, yet one that nevertheless has concrete ramifications for people for whom urban development and demographic change has spawned economic and social marginalization. Ideological assumptions, coupled with social and political interests, are, according to Porter and Shaw (2009), the motivating force behind revitalization projects, which often elevate economic success over the best interests of individuals and communities.

## The Urban Boom

The legacy of urban planning in Vancouver is palpable. Hutton (2004b) argues that Vancouver's contemporary renewal projects are the product of a post-industrialist ideological legacy, largely adopted in the mid-1970s, championed by local politicians eager to accommodate both local and foreign business interests. A wider trend of municipal mega-projects during the same period gave rise to substantial government investments in urban infrastructure including stadiums, subway lines and road maintenance, all intended to propagate a policy of urbanization and the revitalization of North American cities (Altshuler & Luberoff 2003). The transformation of Vancouver's False Creek South community, at the time, exemplified the obsolescence of urban industry and the rise of medium-density, mixed-income residential neighborhoods as places of clustered production and mass consumption. As David Ley (1994, 2003; Ley & Dobson 2008) has suggested, the False Creek project was, at the time, a dramatic metaphor of urban liberalism that sought to promote an ethic of consumption, service and livability. Ley has gone on to argue that the increase of left-liberal middle-class professionals settling in Vancouver has promoted and sustained urban renewal projects celebrated by public officials (particularly internationally) as important, unique examples of urban sustainability.

The post-industrial ideology of urban planning was followed by a renewed attention on residential density in Vancouver when in 1991 the City and its Planning Division introduced Vancouver's Central Area Plan (CAP) (Hutton 2004b). The CAP aimed to consolidate the central business district in order to free space for housing and transform land adjacent to its core into high-end residential and multi-use communities. As a result, the Concord Pacific Place project (False Creek North) and the Granville Slopes (including the Granville Island area) became home to 20,000 new residential units capable of housing upwards of 30,000 additional residents. Hutton observes that while today the central business district remains the largest concentrated area of employment in Vancouver, there is now a "burgeoning mosaic of new service industry clusters which has reconfigured the central city's space-economy and spatial divisions of labor" (2004b, 1967). In other words, semi-autonomous geographic areas, including the transformed False Creek and Granville Island communities, now play host to a variety of industries aimed at promoting increased consumption via the provision of goods and services locally. The promotion of tourism has likewise fueled the development of these neighborhoods, with smaller-scale entertainment districts, including bars and restaurants, supporting an influx of commerce. However, other scholars point out that the increasing co-existence of residential, commercial and even industrial spaces has, in many instances, given rise to new and different challenges including increasing pollution in urban residential areas, increased potential health risks, as well as trends toward ongoing socioeconomic stratification within the urban core (Angotti & Hanhardt 2001). Nevertheless, this model of development has been celebrated and copied both nationally and internationally as a leading model of successful urban renewal and economic development.

Vancouver underwent another urban transformation and regeneration projects when the bid to host the 2010 Winter Olympics gave rise to Project Civil City. Central to this new planning initiative was the reduction of street disorder in the city, particularly in downtown Gastown and Yaletown communities, in an attempt to establish greater social control across the city, with the consequence of increasing social inequality. Boyle and Haggerty (2011) argue that Project Civil City should be seen in the context of the development of Vancouver as an area both for market-oriented economic growth and for elite consumption practices. The Olympics provided an opportunity to accelerate a number of longstanding objectives for the city, including the regulation of disorder. While the actual dislocation, direct intimidation and incarceration of the Vancouver's impoverished populations was limited compared to other Olympic games, such as Atlanta, the fact that many

*Figure 4.3* A truck hauls material to a new luxury condo under construction in Southeast False Creek, Vancouver

Photo by Dan Zuberi

policies and protocols remain in place today (post-Olympics) is a testament to the efforts of City officials keen to preserve the social regulation of space in the city's downtown core. As repeatedly noted in gentrification literature, the dislocation of low-income individuals from urban communities remains a central tenet of revitalization projects (Olagnero & Ballor 2010; Rerat et al. 2010; Schill & Nathan 1983). Major events, such as the 2010 Winter Olympics, provide a catalyst for more timely and permanent changes under the auspices of event hosting and international prestige.

Smith (2007) examines the phenomenon of mega-event planning in the context of urban gentrification, and argues that the planning process around hosting large events exemplifies the epitome of top-down approaches to redevelopment. Their legacy can have lasting impacts on urban spaces and this is often financially straining. A prominent example is Vancouver's Athletes' Village development, for which the City of Vancouver borrowed nearly $500 million CAD from the province in order to finance its completion after the New York investment firm originally contracted went bankrupt. Public outcry sparked intense debate over the appropriate allocation of public

*Figure 4.4* A new urban community is realized with the construction of Vancouver's Olympic Village

Photo by Dan Zuberi

funds and the lack of transparency around the project's completion. Though originally proposed as a mixed income, multi-use space, the City opted to recoup as much financial loss as possible, and so significantly reduced the low-income and public service facilities originally proposed. Vancouver's Athletes' Village development remains an important example of the kind of top-down development scheme criticized by gentrification scholars, and in many ways epitomizes the weaknesses of neoliberal public–private partnerships, where corporations stand to reap immense profits, while the government and public unknowingly shoulders immense risk and ends up paying the price in the event of failure.

## The Potential Bust

Beazley et al. (1997) argue that the phenomenon of top-down development is particularly salient in North American cities as local governments increasingly prioritize pro-growth interests over the needs of disadvantaged communities. Municipal and other governments are increasingly unable or unwilling to organize the kinds of resources required for mega-projects and critical infrastructure upgrades. Meanwhile, these governments are being pushed and pulled toward working with the private sector on urban regeneration and other projects as the only option to accomplish critical policy objectives. The diminishing commitment toward housing low-income individuals in the Vancouver Athlete's Village is a perfect example of how the introduction of private sector actors makes socially desirable benefits vulnerable. Instead, these initiatives privilege the interests and access of economically stable populations and the promotion of consumer markets sustained by them. The prestige associated with urban mega-projects including the Vancouver's Athletes' Village means that the interests of developers are often placed above those of local interest groups or communities, and the interests of developers align with the wealthy and privileged over lower-income and vulnerable populations. These urban regeneration schemes show a growing acceptance of private sector actors and interests as driving urban regeneration in the neoliberal era. We are currently witnessing the evolution or next step of expanding corporate franchise development; IKEA has designed and developed a pre-packaged new urban community for East London. The 26-acre mixed-income development, Strand East, will be built near the Olympic Park and include housing, office space, hotel, and floating cocktail bar. All units will be rented directly from IKEA.

The current model of large-scale urban development is both diverse and flexible; however, Lehrer and Laidley (2008) argue that unlike mega-projects of the past, contemporary approaches exemplify a larger cultural shift from collective to individual needs and benefits. Moreover, in today's global inter-urban competitive landscape, the drive to specialize in everything falsely assumes that all interests are being served, while actually reinforcing traditional divisions. The increasing commodification of urban space may be fueled by demographic and economic changes in cities like Vancouver; however, the parallel circumscription of public space remains at heart a policy issue. Innovations in urban planning practices will have direct impact on the attributes of modern cities and the quality of life that those who live there are able to enjoy.

Increasing investment, growing industry and social upgrading characteristics of the 'new economy' will, according to Mason (2003) put increased pressure on adjacent Vancouver neighborhoods to gentrify, potentially destabilizing those households unable to adapt. Increasing real estate investment and speculation by wealthy individuals internationally is already driving up the luxury real estate market in many global cities, de-linking real estate prices and rents from local economic realities, conditions and trends. Even in a progressive city such as Vancouver, ongoing public investments have marginally assisted in the maintenance of low-income housing options, although quality and size remain at issue, with the downtown neighborhood

*Figure 4.5* Residential towers dominate this Vancouver skyline
Photo by Dan Zuberi

of Gastown experiencing a 225 percent increase in the number of private sector condominium units between 1995 and 2000 with only a 24 percent increase in social housing units over the same period (Mason 2003). Public development and regeneration has been swamped by the effects of global capital flows and neoliberalism.

Carmon and Baron (1994) argue that the gentrification of disadvantaged communities, such as Gastown, occurs through the revitalization of housing and services, which serve as important factors in the popularization of distressed areas. Yet they also point to the reclassification of neighborhood status through pointed marketing campaigns, which have helped to attract an influx of middle-and upper-class households, and provide a central catalyst for community change. The transformation of Vancouver's Gastown neighborhood through targeted cultural branding as much as renovated housing and new developments has reconstituted the social and economic status of the community.

Broader trends have sought to make social inclusion a more prominent force in urban development. However, the extent to which social issues shape outcomes has been questioned by scholars who highlight challenges around integration versus segregation outcomes of mixed-use infrastructure projects and the drive for sustainable communities (Glasson & Wood 2009). Ley and Dobson (2008) however point to examples of stalled gentrification projects in both Vancouver's Downtown Eastside and Grandview-Woodlands communities and argue they are the result of neighborhood political mobilization, cultures of poverty, and an ongoing public policy of social housing. However, declining affordability elsewhere in the city means that middle-income earners are increasingly drawn to these areas resulting in conflicts over the meaning of livability and the ownership over public spaces. As neighborhood demographics begin to shift, we also see shifts in lifestyle, consumption and aesthetic; simultaneously, disadvantaged populations face serious challenges and even displacement.

Chan and Lee (2008) argue that sustainable urban design concepts promote principles of space maximization, conservation of resources and the facilitation of daily needs. However, in reality these factors are not universal and can vary widely by community. Quastel (2009) similarly notes that material relations, uneven resource consumption practices and shifts in population demographics have created a blanket gentrification process that singularly targets desired demographics through the promotion of revitalized neighborhoods as sustainable, modern and 'green.' He argues that the City invokes a strategy of densification in poorer neighborhoods under the auspiciousness of environmental sustainability in a process he terms 'ecological gentrification.' Increasing sensitivities toward environmental impacts of gentrification projects have, according to Orueta and Fainstein

(2008), helped to create more sustainable communities; however, they also suggest the same phenomenon has helped to fuel social exclusion through the promotion of middle and upper-class ethics.

Vancouver's changing urban landscape has led to an increasing trend toward centralized living as people live, work and play largely in the same small area. Consumer demands now prioritize walkability, convenience and quality of amenities in choosing a neighborhood, eliminating long and expensive commutes. Moos and Skaburskis (2007) argue that residential gentrification promotes home-based work/employment and allows for greater locational flexibility within already existing urban clusters. In other words, urban residents increasingly negate workplace concerns when selecting a residence, since their professional needs can be satisfied sufficiently in many different urban communities. The continuing prevalence of work/live spaces in the downtown communities of Yaletown and Gastown further consolidate these areas as self-sustaining. Researchers note however that in Vancouver's affluent urban community of Yaletown, the majority of residents (57 percent) drive to and from work almost daily, despite living and working in the downtown core (Danyluk & Ley 2007; Quastel 2009). Similarly, Vancouver public transit statistics suggest populations moving into the gentrified areas of Yaletown, Gastown and False Creek rely less on city bus and skytrain routes than do other populations and instead walk, cycle or drive regularly (Danyluk & Ley 2007). This may suggest that the 'new economy', and the creative class of young professionals it sustains, reproduces wealth and class in ways that further segregate populations economically and culturally.

Urban regeneration and gentrification in Vancouver has pushed newcomer minority immigrants and refugees into the declining inner-ring suburbs and edge cities, disrupting traditional patterns of center city settlement. As these communities face growing social problems and declining resource bases, these new vulnerable populations face the risk of invisibility and lack of access to critical services and resources.

## Looking Forward

The restructuring of Vancouver's downtown core has created an economic, social, political and ideological space dominated by the new creative professional class (Quastel 2009). Mason (2003) argues that this trend has been the direct result of the interventionist land-reform practices employed by the City of Vancouver and the political agenda of economic stimulation it champions. Indeed, today the municipal government remains the largest landowner citywide and has re-zoned over 8 million square feet [743,224 square meters] of commercial and industrial land for residential use since

1991, helping to densify Vancouver's downtown core. What has changed over the last decade, Mason argues, is Vancouver's position vis-à-vis the globalized economic development market, and the necessity of Vancouver's business and government to remain attractive to international commerce. For example, in contrast to the False Creek projects of the 1970s, more recent developments, such as Southeast False Creek, are championed as international examples of urban sustainability in an effort to attract foreign capital investments. What has also changed is the extensive dependence and involvement of private interests in urban regeneration schemes, with predominantly government-led efforts giving way to partnerships and private sector initiated initiatives.

The proliferation across North American cities of public–private partnerships for the purpose of redevelopment is, according to some, an exercise in empowering private business through the reallocation of public resources and capital. The situation is then exacerbated by political, institutional and partnership constraints that erode the ability of local governments to prioritize community, promote inclusion and make planning decisions that are in the public interest (Erie et al. 2010). Others argue in favor of the public–private partnerships model in the context of declining provincial and federal subsidies for municipal projects. They celebrate the economic revenues generated by mega-projects, and argue that increased affluence in previously disadvantaged neighborhoods helps to boost local economies and revitalize struggling communities (Frieden & Sagalyn 1990; Schill & Nathan 1983). Yet these celebrations ignore the costs, which fall most directly on the most vulnerable and disadvantaged. It is not in the interest of private developers to serve the interests of these groups. They also ignore the shift in the reward/risk nexus; while these schemes are sold as shifting risk to the private sector, in the actual cases of failure, it is the government and public which are left responsible for picking up the tab.

The challenge of researchers and scholars lies in understanding the competing priorities of urban communities and the privileging of one kind of modern lifestyle. What are the broader implications of these changes and how do they contribute to social and economic unrest, equity and rights to the city? While the needs of vulnerable populations were frequently diminished and left unsatisfied in earlier government-led urban regeneration schemes or worse (including bulldozing an estimated 1,600 African-American neighborhoods in the United States as described by Mindy Fullilove in her book *Root Shock* [2004]), the new neoliberal era of public–private partnerships and packaged condo tower urban redevelopments have gone even further in serving the interests of the elite, and contributing to growing social exclusion and inequality in urban centers.

## Conclusion

Gentrification projects continue to challenge, redefine and upset the status quo of North American cities. This chapter has argued that global neoliberal policies and practices increasingly drive the nature of urban regeneration, accelerating the vulnerability of and displacement of the economically disadvantaged. Vancouver, Canada, serves as an important and unique case study of urban regeneration as it has helped to support a demographic and cultural shift in residential and consumer demand. Concerns about environmental sustainability, the provision and consumption of services, and the changing nature of work have each contributed to shifting patterns of urban regeneration. At the same time, larger political and economic trends and growing importance of globalization cannot be ignored. The legacy of mega-events remains an important determinant of city planning initiatives and urban regeneration. The growing reliance on the private sector has resulted in a declining commitment to the public good, as urban regeneration is increasing driven by the interests of developers and the global elite. Promoting the livability of North America's urban cores is likely to continue concurrent with urban regeneration, but the social tensions unearthed through ongoing dislocation and economic strain will also continue to challenge planners and policymakers to envision a more diverse, inclusive and socially sustainable future for urban living. Most importantly, there need to be new mechanisms introduced to represent the interests of the public, particularly the economically disadvantaged, so as to counter the general trend of growing social exclusion, dislocation and disenfranchisement in the global city.

## References

Allen, C. (2008) *Housing Market Renewal and Social class*. London: Routledge.
Altshuler, A., and Luberoff, D.E. (2003) *Mega-Projects: The Changing Politics of Urban Public Investment*. Washington: Brookings Institution Press.
Angotti, T., and Eva, H. (2001) "Problems and Prospects for Healthy Mixed-Use Communities in New York City", *Planning Practice & Research*, 16(2): 145–154.
Barnes, T., and Hutton, T. (2009) "Situating the New Economy: Contingencies of Regeneration and Dislocation in Vancouver's Inner City", *Urban Studies*, 46(5–6): 1247–1269.
Beazley, M., Loftman, P., and Nevin, B. (1997) "Downtown Redevelopment and Community Resistance: An International Perspective", In N. Jewson and S. MacGregor (eds.), *Transforming Cities: Contested Governance and New Spatial Divisions*. London: Routledge.
Boyle, P., and Haggerty, K. (2011) "Civil Cities and Urban Governance Regulation: Disorder for the Vancouver Winter Olympics", *Urban Studies*, 48(15): 3185–3320.

Brenner, N., and Theodore, N. (eds.). (2003) *Spaces of Neoliberalism: Urban Restructuring in North America and Europe*. Oxford: Blackwell Publishing.

Bright, E.M. (2000) *Reviving America's Forgotten Neighborhoods: An Investigation of Inner City Revitalization Efforts*. New York: Garland.

Carmon, N., and Baron, M. (1994) "Reducing Inequality by Means of Neighborhood Rehabilitation: An Israeli Experience and Its Lessons", *Urban Studies*, 31(9): 1465–1479.

Chan, E., and Lee, G.K.L. (2008) "Critical Factors for Improving the Social Sustainability of Urban Renewal Projects", *Social Indicators Research*, 85(2): 243–256.

Danyluk, M., and Ley, D. (2007) "Modalities of the New Middle Class: Ideology and Behaviour in the Journey to Work from Gentrified Neighbourhoods in Canada", *Urban Studies*, 44(11): 2195–2210.

Davidson, M., and Lees, L. (2010) "New-Build Gentrification: Its Histories, Trajectories, and Critical Geographies", *Population, Space and Place*, 16(5): 395–411.

Erie, S.P., Kogan, V., and MacKenzie, S.A. (2010) "Redevelopment, San Diego Style: The Limits of Public–Private Partnerships", *Urban Affairs Review*, 45(5): 644–678.

Florida, R. (2003) *The Rise of the Creative Class: And How It's Transforming Work, Leisure, Community, and Daily Life*. New York: Basic Books.

Frieden, B.J., and Sagalyn, L.B. (1990) *Downtown Inc.: How America Rebuilds Cities*. Boston: MIT Press.

Fullilove, M. (2004). *Root Shock: How Tearing Up City Neighborhoods Hurts America and What We Can Do about It*. New York: Ballantine Books.

Glasson, J., and Wood, G. (2009) "Urban Regeneration and Impact Assessment for Social Sustainability", *Impact Assessment and Project Appraisal*, 27(4): 283–290.

Hutton, T.A. (2004a) "The New Economy of the Inner City", *Cities*, 21(2): 89–108.

Hutton, T. (2004b) "Post-Industrialism, Post-Modernism and the Reproduction of Vancouver's Central Area: Re-Theorizing the 21st Century City", *Urban Studies*, 41(10): 1953–1982.

Hutton, T.A. (2008) *The New Economy of the Inner city: Restructuring, Regeneration and Dislocation in the Twenty-First-Century Metropolis*. London: Routledge.

Lehrer, U., and Laidley, J. (2008) "Old Mega-Projects Newly Packaged? Waterfront Redevelopment in Toronto", *International Journal of Urban and Regional Research*, 32(4): 786–803.

Ley, D. (1994) "Gentrification and the Politics of the New Middle Class", *Environment and Planning D*, 12(1): 53–74.

Ley, D. (1997) *The New Middle Class and the Remaking of the Central City*. Oxford: Oxford University Press.

Ley, D. (2003) "Artists, Aestheticisation and the Field of Gentrification", *Urban Studies*, 40(12): 2527–2544.

Ley, D., and Dobson, C. (2008) "Are There Limits to Gentrification? The Contexts of Impeded Gentrification in Vancouver", *Urban Studies*, 45(12): 2471–2498.

Mason, M. (2003) "Urban Regeneration Rationalities and Quality of Life: Comparative Notes from Toronto, Montreal and Vancouver", *British Journal of Canadian Studies*, 16(2): 348–362.

Meligrana, J., and Skaburskis, A. (2005) "Extent, Location and Profiles of Continuing Gentrification in Canadian Metropolitan Areas 1981–2001", *Urban Studies*, 42(9): 1569–1592.

Metro Vancouver. (2012) *Census Demographic Bulletin and Maps*. Online. www. metrovancouver.org/about/statistics/Pages/CensusBulletins.aspx [last accessed 21 March 2012].

Moos, M., and Skaburskis, A. (2007) "The Characteristics and Location of Homeworkers in Montreal, Toronto and Vancouver", *Urban Studies*, 44: 1781–1808.

Olagnero, M., and Ballor, F. (2010) "Living and Cooperating in a Housing Mix Neighbourhood: The Olympic Villages 'Torino 2006': A Case Study", *Rassegna Italiana di Sociologia*, 3: 429–458.

Orueta, F.D., and Fainstein, S.S. (2008) "The New Mega-Projects: Genesis and Impacts", *International Journal of Urban and Regional Research*, 32(4): 759–767.

Pollard, J.S. (2004) "From Industrial District to Urban Village? Manufacturing, Money and Consumption in Birminghams Jewellery Quarter", *Urban Studies*, 41(1): 173–193.

Porter, L., and Shaw, K. (eds.). (2009) *Whose Urban Renaissance? An International Comparison of Urban Regeneration Strategies*. New York: Routledge.

Punter, J. (2003) *The Vancouver Achievement: Urban Planning and Design*. Vancouver: UBC Press.

Quastel, N. (2009) "Political Ecologies of Gentrification", *Urban Geography*, 30(7): 694–725.

Rerat, P., Soderstrom, O., and Piguet, E. (2010) "New Forms of Gentrification: Issues and Debates", *Population, Space and Place*, 16(5): 335–343.

Schill, M.H., and Nathan, R.P. (1983) *Revitalizing America's Cities: Neighborhood Reinvestment and Displacement*. New York: SUNY Press.

Smith, A. (2007) "Large-Scale Events and Sustainable Urban Regeneration: Key Principles for Host Cities", *Journal of Urban Regeneration and Renewal*, 1(2): 178–190.

Squires, G. (1989) *Unequal Partnerships: The Political Economy of Urban Redevelopment in Postwar America*. New Brunswick, NJ: Rutgers University Press.

Walks, A., and Maaranen, R. (2008) "From Gentrification to Social Mix, or Social Polarization?: Testing the Claims in Large Canadian Cities", *Urban Geography*, 29(4): 293–326.

# 5 Urban Regeneration in North America Today
## Outcomes, Trends and Future Challenges

Having examined trends in social-spatial inequality across a number of North American cities—including those facilitated by mega-project development, social housing and brownfield cleanup—we now step back and reflect on broader contemporary trends in urban regeneration. Processes of suburbanization, deindustrialization and neoliberalism have transformed both the physical and sociological infrastructure and demographics of urban cores across North America. While in some cities the recent influx of an educated and high-earning creative class has brought with it renewed investment in urban mega-projects and inspired more livable urban design, many major metropolitan areas continue to experience escalating inequality and enduring high rates of concentrated poverty. In the United States, between 2000 and 2009, the number of extremely poor neighborhoods grew by over 40 percent. By 2014, nearly 14 million Americans lived in neighborhoods with poverty rates of 40 percent or more (Kneebone & Holmes 2016). While cities continue to experience a renaissance in urban renewal, the socioeconomic benefits have not been equitably distributed.

In cities across North America, low-income housing has been replaced by mixed-use and market-driven alternatives that pathologize the lives of many long-time residents. New tough-on-crime and zero-tolerance policing work to redefine public spaces as places of leisure and consumption is reserved for those who can afford to participate. At the same time, the pressures of gentrification continue to push many low-income families out of urban cores and into peripheral and often under-serviced suburban areas. While brownfields once offered a degree of economic reprieve for low-income urban residents, lasting sociological and environmental impacts are significant. Today, in the context of growing public support for environmental sustainability, brownfields are finally being targeted for cleanup, yet the piecemeal and market-driven approach to brownfield regeneration has brought with it all the challenges of sociological and economic gentrification, particularly when they are located in desirable urban areas such as waterfronts.

*Figure 5.1*  A San Francisco Juvenile Justice Center represents the expansion of the
incarceral state

Photo by Dan Zuberi

Paradoxically, the pursuit of sustainability and 'green' solutions to urban
development that continues to drive the increase in brownfield cleanup has,
under conditions of neoliberal economics, largely failed to address sociological concerns. As a result, conceptualizations of sustainability routinely
fall short of achieving equitable or just outcomes for many who have long
relied on blue-collar forms of employment.

These broader trends are however not isolated to the North American
cities explored in the preceding chapters. Poverty rates continue to rise in
most major metropolitan areas on both sides of the U.S.–Canada border.
The 2008–2009 global recession has only served to exacerbate this trend,
the consequences of which have been notably more severe in the United
States as opposed to Canada. Despite the recovery, a recent study found that
among the 71 largest U.S. cities, 59 continue to face poverty levels higher
than pre-recession levels. Moreover, 68 of these cities are now home to
significantly larger populations, and today, 16 now host at least 50 percent
more low-income families than in 2007 (Kneebone & Holmes 2015).

*Figure 5.2*  A living wall in San Francisco adds green aesthetic to apartment complex
Photo by Dan Zuberi

Household income inequality is also growing. While high-income house-holds did earn less on average in 2014 than in 2007 in 33 of the hundred largest U.S. cities, the same was also true for low-income households in 81 (Berube & Holmes 2016). Moreover, in cities where inequality is highest, housing for low-income households remains least affordable, particularly when so many jobs remain low-wage. In 2012, the U.S. Bureau of Labor Statistics reported the creation of 6 million new jobs in just a 2-year period, yet these jobs have not directly benefited those most in need. According to a recent study by the Working Poor Families Project, the number of low-income American families (those making less than $22,811 for a family of four with two children) actually rose from 8 to 11 percent between 2007 and 2011. Lower-wage jobs (those paying between $7.69 and $13.83 per hour) continue to make up the vast majority of post-recession job growth across the United States. Not only are these jobs low paying, but they are also increasingly temporary (Rasheed 2013, 6–7).

The story is somewhat different in the Canadian urban setting, despite many overarching similarities. Scholars generally agree that Canadian cit-ies have largely avoided the ghettoized and racialized enclaves of poverty long present in the United States (Fong 1996; Ley & Smith 1997; Walks &

Bourne 2006; Stranger-Ross & Ross 2012, 214). However, recent work has warned of rising concentrations of urban poverty in Canada's largest cities (Toronto, Vancouver and Montreal), brought on by many of trends explored throughout this book (Fong & Shibuya 2000, 2003; Kazempiur & Halli 2000). It is significant that even long-time skeptics now admit: "Even if Toronto is not yet Detroit, we might still have grounds for concern" (Stranger-Ross & Ross 2012, 213–214).

Part of the challenge of comparing American and Canadian urban poverty lies in the diversity of measurement tools employed to capture national-level trends. Canada lacks an official poverty line, and unlike the United States, three separate statistical measures are disparately used. Statistics Canada's Low-Income Cutoff (LICO) is the most widely employed and provides an important threshold below which families must allocate a larger percentage of earnings to necessities relative to the Canadian average. By contrast, the Low-Income Measure (LIM) and the Marked-Basket Measure (MBM) are generated for international comparisons by using a fixed percentage of income and a basket of essential goods and services. However, critics have long argued that the LICO fails to take into account variations in the cost of living regionally, while others argue the LIM and MBM are subject to manipulation based on what items are (or are not) included in the economic basket (MacKinnon 2013). However, despite these differences, according to even the lowest commonly accepted measure, nearly 3 million Canadians are currently living in poverty, the vast majority of whom reside in major urban centers (Shields et al. 2011, 103).

In both Canada and the United States, race and ethnicity also continue to be strongly associated with poverty, particularly in urban areas. In 2003, poverty rates among American blacks and Hispanics were 24.3 percent and 22.5 percent respectively, while just 8.2 percent for white American.

*Table 5.1*  The number of Canadian families living in poverty has increased across urban areas.

| Low-Income Cut-Offs (1992 Base) After TaxBased on Family of Four | | | | | | |
|---|---|---|---|---|---|---|
| Census Metropolitan Area (CMA) | 1992 | 1996 | 2000 | 2004 | 2008 | 2011 |
| Between 100,000 and 499,999 inhabitants | 21,628 | 22,890 | 24,563 | 26,958 | 29,378 | 30,871 |
| 500,000 or more | 25,574 | 27,066 | 29,045 | 31,876 | 34,738 | 36,504 |

Source: Statistics Canada, www.statcan.gc.ca/pub/75f0002m/2012002/tbl/tbl01-eng.htm

Immigrants to the United States are disproportionately prone to poverty at a rate of 17.4 percent (Hoynes et al. 2006, 49). In Canada, the spatialized concentration of low-income earners also tends to occur in immigrant-dominated communities. These neighborhoods are also increasingly subur-ban, as rising costs of living in city cores continues to push these populations

*Figure 5.3*  Towers along Vancouver's False Creek, built to accommodate growing population demands

Photo by Dan Zuberi

into more affordable peripheral areas that often lack adequate housing and transport infrastructure (Shields et al. 2011, 95–96). And while the national rate of poverty among newly arrived immigrants to Canada is extreme (45 percent), Montreal, Vancouver and Toronto shoulder the vast majority of newcomers and, in turn, the challenges associated with their socioeconomic integration (Shields et al. 2011, 104).

That poverty has increased in both Canada and the United States since 2000 is perhaps not in and of itself surprising. After all, the global financial crisis, declining manufacturing and social welfare retrenchment are familiar challenges facing population on both sides of the border. Yet, the uneven distribution of poverty between urban centers and within urban communities is notable. For example, in the United States, the national poverty rate rose by 3.2 percentage points between 2000 and 2010, yet census tracts have not been equally impacted. Between 2010 and 2014, America's 100 largest metropolitan areas "remained home to more than 70 percent of all poor individuals living in extremely poor neighborhoods" (Kneebone & Holmes 2016).

In Canada, urban areas have also grown in population, despite declining average incomes. There has been an increase in precarious and part-time work in Canada, with many newly created jobs offering low-wages, limited benefits and poor job security. Toronto experienced the most significant decline in terms of average wages of any of the largest metropolitan areas in the country, with median incomes declining by 4.2 percent in just a 10-year period (MacDonnell et al. 2004, 14).

At the same time, income inequality has also expanded and is most stark in urban centers. Toronto and Vancouver have experienced the sharpest division among high and low-income earners with only Montreal falling below the national average. The loss of well-paid manufacturing jobs helps to partially explain this trend. For example, 73,213 manufacturing jobs were lost in the city of Toronto between 1983 and 2003, a 30 percent decline. At the same time, as wages fell, the cost of living has continued to climb. Rising real estate

*Table 5.2* Changes in Median Income for Canadian Census Families, Canada and Large CMAs, 1990–2000 (constant $2000)

| | MEDIAN INCOME ($) | | % CHANGE |
|---|---|---|---|
| | 1990 | 2000 | 1990–2000 |
| CANADA | 54,560 | 55,016 | 0.8 |
| MONTREAL | 53,624 | 53,385 | −0.4 |
| TORONTO | 66,520 | 63,700 | −4.2 |
| CALGARY | 61,408 | 65,488 | 6.6 |
| VANCOUVER | 60,254 | 57,926 | −3.9 |

Source: Statistics Canada, www.statcan.gc.ca/pub/75f0002m/2012002/tbl/tbl01-eng.htm

prices and increasing rents in light of low vacancy rates require an increasing share of the income of both owners and renters. Data from the 2001 Canadian census reveal that at the time, 197,270 tenets faced rental rates demanding 30 percent or more of their earnings (MacDonnell et al. 2004, 14).

In the United States, a recent study found the ratio of the 90th to the 10th wage percentile has also increased between 2003 and 2013 by a rate of 7 percent. According to U.S. Bureau of Labor, the highest paid 10th percentile of wage earners earned at least $88,330 USD in 2013, while the lowest paid 10 percent earned less than $18,190 USD annually. Real annual wages have, over the same time period, actually increased for the highest paid workers and decreased for those in the lowest paid positions (Bureau of Labor Statistics 2015). While 2014 data from the U.S. Internal Revenue Service show a 3.3 percent increase in earnings over 2013 levels for those in the bottom 99 percent, incomes for those in the top 1 percent of earners grew by 10.8 percent over the same period (Saez 2015). It is indeed notable that today more than half jobs in the United States pay less than $34,000 USD per year, and this represents an increase of just 7 percent since 1973 (Rasheed 2013, 7).

Municipal level data only serve to confirm many of these wider trends. In many of North America's largest cities, poverty remains serious challenge

*Figure 5.4* New York real estate prices and rents continue to soar especially in the wealthy Upper Eastside

Photo by Dan Zuberi

for many individuals and families who face rising living costs and depressed incomes. Processes of gentrification continue to push many people out of communities they have long occupied as affordable housing options decline. According to U.S. census data, the median value of an owner-occupied housing unit in New York City between 2010–2014 was $490,700. By contrast, the median household income in New York City over the same period was just $52,737 (U.S. Census Bureau 2016). High and increasing real estate prices and rents in many U.S. cities have contributed to high rates of housing insecurity and stress for lower-income individuals and families, exacerbating social-spatial polarization and now gentrification pressures in low-income neighborhoods.

It is little wonder that suburban poverty is also growing. As low-income earners are no longer able to meet the rising cost associated in the city, they are pushed to peripheral areas that often ethnically segregated and can lack the same quality of services such as public transportation (Shields et al. 2011, 95–96). Within many of America's largest cities, concentrated poverty has emerged well beyond urban cores. In the last decade, the number of suburban poor has almost doubled, with post-recession rates increasing

*Figure 5.5* In New York City, book vendors set up on city streets

Photo by Dan Zuberi

from 2.4 to 7.1 percentage points (Kneebone & Holmes 2016). Yet while the number of suburban poor is certainly increasing, cities remain home to roughly three-quarters (74 percent) of extreme poverty neighborhoods in the United States (Kneebone & Holmes 2016).

Throughout this book, we have aimed to show how seemingly disparate development strategies come together to reproduce (and even exacerbate) existing forms of social and spatial inequality across North American cities. Mega-project development, social housing development and the greening of urban brownfield land are each driven in part by wider normative and political commitments to neoliberal economic restructuring and the democratic deficit that supports and reproduces it. While participatory planning practices have begun to emerge, they struggle to make real inroads in a context where market-driven valuations of people and property prevail. In the final chapter, we revisit many of the lessons captured in previous chapters and attempt to apply them to a number of policy recommendations we see as fundamental to the pursuit of more equitable, inclusive and just urban communities.

## References

Berube, A., and Holmes, N. (2016) "City and Metropolitan Inequality on the Rise, Driven by Declining Income", *The Bookings Institute*. Published 14 January 2016. www.brookings.edu/research/city-and-metropolitan-inequality-on-the-rise-driven-by-declining-incomes/ [last accessed 13 March 2017].

Bureau of Labor Statistics. (2015) "Measuring Wage Inequalities within and across U.S. Metropolitan Areas, 2003–2013", *U.S. Department of Labor*. Published September 2015. www.bls.gov/opub/mlr/2015/article/measuring-wage-inequality-within-and-across-metropolitan-areas-2003-13.htm [last accessed 13 March 2017].

Fong, E. (1996) "A Comparative Perspective on Racial Residential Segregation: American and Canadian Experiences", *Sociological Quarterly*, 37: 199–226.

Fong, E., and Shibuya, K. (2000) "The Spatial Separation of the Poor in Canadian Cities", *Demography*, 37: 449–459.

Fong, E., and Shibuya, K. (2003) "Economic Changes in Canadian Neighborhoods", *Population Research and Policy Review*, 22: 147–170.

Hoynes, H.W., Page, M.E., and Stevens, H.F. (2006) "Poverty in America: Trends and Explanations", *Journal of Economic Perspectives*, 20: 47–68.

Kazempiur, A., and Halli, S.S. (2000) "Neighbourhood Poverty in Canadian Cities", *Canadian Journal of Sociology*, 25: 369–381.

Kneebone, E., and Holmes, N. (2015) "New Census Data Finds Scant Progress against Poverty", *The Brooking Institute*. Published 18 September 2015. www.brookings.edu/blog/the-avenue/2015/09/18/new-census-data-finds-scant-progress-against-poverty/ [last accessed 13 March 2017].

Kneebone, E., and Holmes, N. (2016) "US Concentrated Poverty in the Wake of the Great Recession", *The Brookings Institute*. Published 31 March 2016.

www.brookings.edu/research/u-s-concentrated-poverty-in-the-wake-of-the-great-recession/ [last accessed 13 March 2017].

Ley, D., and Smith, H. (1997) "Is There an Immigrant 'Underclass' in Canadian Cities?", Working Paper 97–08, Research on Immigration and Integration in the Metropolis, Working Paper Series, Vancouver Centre for Excellence, Simon Fraser University.

MacDonnell, S., Embuldeniya, D., and Ratanshi, F. (2004) *Poverty by Postal Code: The Geography of Neighbourhood Poverty, City of Toronto, 1981–2001*. Toronto: United Way.

MacKinnon, S. (2013) "The Politics of Poverty in Canada", *Social Alternatives*, 32: 19–23.

Rasheed, M. (2013) "A Brief Look at Poverty in America", *Journal of Housing and Community Development*, 70(2): 6–7.

Saez, E. (2015) "US Income Inequality Persists amidst Overall Growth in 2014", *Washington Center for Equitable Growth*. Published 29 June 2015. http://equitablegrowth.org/research-analysis/u-s-income-inequality-persists-amid-overall-growth-2014/ [last accessed 13 March 2017].

Shields, J., Kelly, P., Park, S., Prier, N., and Fang, T. (2011) "Profiling Immigrant Poverty in Canada: A 2006 Census Statistical Portrait", *Canadian Review of Social Policy*, 65–66: 92–111.

Stranger-Ross, J., and Ross, H.S. (2012) "Placing the Poor: The Ecology of Poverty in Postwar Urban Canada", *Journal of Canadian Studies*, 46: 213–240.

U.S. Census Bureau. (2016) "Quick Facts, New York City, New York", *U.S. Department of Commerce*. www.census.gov/quickfacts/table/PST045215/3651000 [last accessed 13 March 2017].

Walks, A., and Bourne, L.S. (2006) "Ghettoes in Canadian Cities? Racial Segregation, Ethnic Enclaves, and Poverty Concentration in Canadian Urban Areas", *Canadian Geographer*, 50(2): 273–297.

# 6 Conclusion and Recommendations

North American cities are experiencing a new and unique stage of regeneration and development, heavily influenced by neoliberalism and tensions between economic growth, equity, promoting diversity, inclusion, as well as government investment and retrenchment. We are deeply concerned with how these forces have changed urban development and renewal patterns, bringing us into the era of the condo-boom. The new era may well be an urban renaissance for some, but it is also a continued and perhaps even greater period of disruption, social exclusion and displacement for others. The neoliberal era of urban regeneration has been facilitated by the confluence of technological integration of a global marketplace and the increasingly service and consumer-based economy of Western countries. Yet, neoliberalism has not so much reduced the scope of government intervention, but rather transformed the nature of legal, political and economic decision making to both facilitate and encourage the growth of private sector activity. The implications have certainly been economic, but they are also social and spatial.

At the level of cities, the achievement of 'smart growth' and 'livable' urban communities have left policymakers less willing and perhaps able to provide the conditions necessary to promote citizen equality. Yet, growing levels of socioeconomic inequality within North American cities in turn raises questions about both the quality and scope of citizen publics in the context of democratic political decision making. The idea that municipal councilors should first and foremost use their resources, not to fight poverty, but to advance corporate and financial interests that, in the context of inter-city competition, may choose to relocate to more business-friendly locales has today become all too widely accepted (Hackworth 2007, 2). In short, neoliberalism, for many scholars, continues to raise important concerns about the democratic capacity of many low-income citizens to overcome the ascendant power of capital in the governance of public life (Hardt & Negri 2004; Dryzek 1996; Bowles & Gintis 1986).

As Jonas and McCarthy argue, cities are increasingly promoting "growth first" or "growth at all costs" rather than fulfilling their democratic obligations to citizens (2010, 33–24). The Entrepreneurial or Competitive City, the Creative City, the Revanchist City and finally the Just City are all theoretical attempts to both diagnose and come to terms with the changing nature of urban life. Recent work by Hackworth (2007), Leitner et al.

*Figure 6.1* Condo towers in San Francisco's downtown core
Photo by Dan Zuberi

(2007), Purcell (2008), Bridge et al. (2012) and others have all made important contributions that work to demystify processes of neoliberal urban restructuring. Promoting the equitable access to, and livability of, urban cores means confronting the dislocation and homogenization that stems from neoliberal governance strategies and taking steps to mitigate this harm.

*Figure 6.2* The bustling streets near Union Square in New York City
Photo by Dan Zuberi

In this final chapter, we revisit some of the findings from previous chapters before presenting a number of creative and innovative policy recommendations to support improved urbanism and urban regeneration in the North American context. These recommendations include investments in accessible social housing, participatory planning initiatives and inclusive public spaces, with the goal of mitigating the dislocations caused by neoliberal urban regeneration and promoting a just and inclusive city as the North American city of the future.

Despite historical differences in socioeconomic policy, we find that in both the United States and Canada, increasing socioeconomic pressure and polarization is routinely associated with urbanization. Gentrification, or the physical displacement of low-income by higher-income populations, is generated through the competitiveness of urban planning under conditions of neoliberal restructuring. By fostering creative and competitive urban communities, we have lost sight of the importance of generating employment and secure living situations for those who are not a part of the creative, financial, professional or economically privileged elites. Yet, at the same time, while urban regeneration has more often than not opened the door to gentrification, we largely agree with Porter and Shaw (2009) that the two are not synonymous, and nor is the later an inevitable result of the former. Ensuring that low-income populations are adequately represented, and their interests amply understood and valued in decision making, is an important first step.

In the first substantive chapter on mega-project development, we showed that it is not simply the realization of equitable access to urban spaces that neoliberal mega-project developments inhibit. As Bornstein and Leetmaa point out, it is simultaneously the exclusion of urban populations from the planning process and the "uneven distribution of publically created value" that neoliberal planning creates (2015, 34). By emphasizing the New Urbanist design principles and the social-spatial reorganization created by Boston's Big Dig and New York City's High Line, we highlighted how actually existing neoliberal regeneration can, despite notable efforts at consultation and mitigation, rapidly gentrify surrounding areas and produce substantial challenges for pre-existing urban communities.

Yet, as San Francisco's Bayview/Hunters Point experience suggests, mega-project development, even in the context of extreme income inequality, is perhaps not inevitably displacing. Instead, it is the all-to-frequent lack of public transparency, accountability and willingness to cooperate and even compensate impacted communities, particularly those most vulnerable to the pressures of gentrification that continues to characterize mega-project regeneration. Mega-projects remain a fixture of the contemporary urban landscape, which raises important questions about their role in facilitating dislocation, social exclusion and the disenfranchisement of low-income populations. More attention must be given to the democratic deficits inherent in the pursuit and realization of mega-project development, particularly given the increasingly privatized and non-transparent governance structures associated with P3 project designs.

In many ways, the exclusion of low-income communities from political decision making has been supported by a shift among policymakers, and indeed some scholars, away from tackling the causes of concentrated urban poverty and toward the pathologization of those individuals living in poverty. Contemporary trends in urban social-spatial inequality across North America remain the legacy of postwar urban renewal projects, but are also sustained by the ongoing stigmatization of urban poverty. A growing body of critical scholarship now shows how the regulation and securitization of urban public space is achieved through the criminalization of anti-social or unwelcome behavior (Madanipour 2010; O'Grady et al. 2013; Chesnay et al. 2013; Kohn 2013). Moreover the privatization of urban public spaces, including parks and promenades, have also worked to regulate life in urban cores, transforming spaces once associated with the formation of social capital into liabilities and untapped sources of profit in an evolving marketplace (Madanipour 2010).

In Chapter 2, we explored how the stigmatization of urban poverty is compounded by the realization of so-called livable urban spaces. As urbanization is fueled by an influx of high-earning, well-educated individuals working in creative industries and other growing sectors (finance, research, etc.), urban cores are being transformed to meet growing consumer demands. The proliferation in mixed-use, mixed-income housing developments is an important example of how the stigmatization of urban poverty has been transformed under conditions of neoliberalism. In the context of decreased funding for social housing, advocates of social mix continue to argue that private sector investment in depressed neighborhoods not only physically revitalizes communities badly in need of investment, but also improves the life chances of low-income residents.

Without ignoring the real problems that exist with social housing developments on both sides of the U.S.–Canada border, we join those scholars who argue for a more nuanced perspective on the effects of low-income residency (August & Walks 2012; James 2010; Laakso 2013 DeFilippis & Wyly 2008). Theoretical perspectives that privilege individual, as opposed to structural, determinants of poverty, have supported projects like HOPE VI and Regent Park, which have been pursued at the expense of dislocation, disrupting important social networks and other sources of social capital. Today a normative consensus among policymakers not only privileges a particular social, racial and class-based ideology, but also prioritizes consumption and entrepreneurship over and above commitments to social justice, equality and citizen participation. While important differences remain between HOPE VI and Regent Park, including the right to return and one-to-one replacement of low-income units, the individualization of poverty, and the pathological behavior it ostensibly spawns, ignores political and economic policies that are deeply implicated in its creation.

We join a growing number of critics who contend that private investment in social housing developments, and indeed the mix of market and

*Figure 6.3* The CN Tower and condominiums overlook a waterfront park in downtown Toronto

Photo by Dan Zuberi

non-market rates associated with mixed occupancy, legitimizes what is in fact a 'false choice' between ongoing neglect of low-income communities and their all but inevitable gentrification (August 2014; DeFilippis 2004; Slater 2006). We lend support to Fainstein's argument that significant increases in affordable housing should be governed by a perpetuity in the affordable housing pool or be subject to one-to-one replacement and that

*Figure 6.4* Mixed-housing at Toronto's Regent Park
Photo by Dan Zuberi

involuntary relocation of households or businesses should be ceased and voluntary movement adequately compensated (2010, 172–173).

Finally, despite many of the structural barriers associated with neoliberal restructuring, we find considerable potential in the participatory planning process pursued in Seattle, WA. The approach adopted by municipal planners in Seattle highlights how citizenship engagement can help to overcome many of the challenges associated top-down-planning initiatives by fostering a sense of inclusiveness, empowerment and ownership over the future of a community. Ensuring citizens have both the political and financial capacity to participate effectively in planning processes allows for a wider variety of perspectives and concerns to be heard and ultimately addressed. In pursuit of a more Just City model of urban life, participatory practices must be augmented by a political commitment to foster more equitable, inclusive and affordable urban communities.

While the strategy in Seattle helped to pioneer a sustainability-centered approach to urban planning, our chapter on brownfield regeneration raises important questions about the sociological dimensions of sustainable urban design. Now a celebrated component of many Smart Growth urban initiatives, we argue that brownfield sites should be understood within the

*Figure 6.5* Public art brightens the streets of San Francisco's Mission District
Photo by Dan Zuberi

broader context of neoliberal urbanization and the gentrification of urban communities. Increasing sensitivities toward the environmental impacts of gentrification projects have, according to Orueta and Fainstein (2008), helped to create more sustainable communities; however, they also suggest the same phenomenon has helped to fuel social exclusion through the promotion of middle- and upper-class ethics. While governments must work to attract investment in contaminated brownfield areas, they must also ensure that land use remains connected to broader community needs. As governments have increasingly embraced strategies for sustainability and committed funds to promote environmental cleanup, many of the social-spatial inequalities associated with gentrification are routinely reproduced.

We find that the development of brownfield land remains fragmented and driven almost exclusively by market forces. In other words, while support for Smart Growth initiatives in both Canada and the United States are part of wider public sustainability planning, brownfields are developed on a parcel-by-parcel basis at the discretion of private investors (Eisen 2009, 10286–10287). At the same time, brownfields disproportionately impact low-income, racialized or otherwise disenfranchised communities, and therefore pose serious challenges for the achievement of spatial and social equity (McCarthy 2009, 226). In the context of the neoliberal city, the exploitation of brownfields for primarily their economic and aesthetic potential raises important questions about how brownfields contribute to wider processes of gentrification and social inequity.

Integrating meaningful community participation and even ownership into urban brownfield development strategies may help to mitigate harm, but without government oversight and intervention, brownfield sites will continue to respond to market forces and directly shape the social-spatial inequalities of urban communities. We find that while the threat of dislocation remains substantial, some communities have begun to demand a vision of sustainability that includes not only environmental, but also social considerations.

In Chapter 4, we find that the case of Vancouver helps to illustrate that while questions of access and rights to the city continue to be part of the dialogue, the solutions are now decidedly more balanced toward public–private partnerships and other market-oriented approaches. Growing concerns about the social and economic impacts of urban communities have ignited discussions of, and resistance to, the monopolization of urban space by privileged groups and the systematic exclusion of disadvantaged communities, many of whom have long occupied contemporary sites of urban gentrification practices. The diminishing commitment toward housing low-income individuals in Vancouver Athlete's Village is a perfect example of how the introduction of private sector actors makes socially desirable benefits vulnerable. Instead, these initiatives privilege the interests and access of economically stable populations and the promotion of consumer markets sustained by them. The top-down approach to urban regeneration is certainly not unique to Vancouver, and many of the outcomes could have been predicted based on the broader urban regeneration literature explored here. We find that Vancouver both exemplifies and challenges prominent themes and observations of urban renewal and adds to our understanding of the changing cityscape through its unique demographic and cultural trajectory.

Cities provide important sites of economic growth, cultural production and consumption practices for a metropolitan region. Yet the notably undemocratic, exclusionary production of new spaces has been repeatedly invoked as the driving force behind urban unrest and volatility through direct and indirect displacement of vulnerable populations (Pollard 2004; Rerat et al. 2010). There is a need for new mechanisms to represent the interests of the public, particularly the economically disadvantaged, so as to counter the general trend of growing social exclusion, dislocation and disenfranchisement in the global city. We propose a number of concrete policy reforms that serve to better represent the interests of low-income populations and to foster more equitable, democratic and inclusively diverse urban spaces.

- Income inequality remains a significant impediment to the realization of a just city alternative. Minimum wage rates on both sides of the U.S.–Canada border have not kept pace with inflation or the rising cost of living associated with urban locales. While U.S. cities including Seattle, along with states such as California and New York, are gradually phasing in a $15/hour minimum wage, the U.S national minimum remains $7.25/hour. While the situation in Canada is relatively more equal, provincial minimum wage rates (currently between $10 and $12 per hour) provide inadequate incomes given high costs of living in major Canadian cities.
- A lack of adequate affordable housing remains one of the largest and most challenging barriers to a just city alternative. A boom in residential demand has facilitated substantive increases in property values, further pricing many lower-income populations out of urban marketplaces. Ensuring that a healthy stock of subsidized low-income housing remains both accessible and desirable for urban populations is key to curbing the social-spatial dislocation brought on by neoliberal urban planning. Policymakers must overcome the false choice between the ongoing degradation of existing social housing and the gentrification inherent in market-based alternatives. Brownfield land offers a significant and under-utilized opportunity to add to the affordable housing stock across many North American cities. However, municipal planners must take steps to integrate brownfields into area-wide planning processes that take seriously the need for non-market rate housing.

- Area-wide planning should provide the structural and financial support to facilitate meaningful public input and participation. Too often the private interests of developers drive land-use planning, which leaves little room for the consideration of existing communities. While many community groups have made important contributions to neighbourhood development plans, more powerful actors too often eclipse their voices. Establishing clear avenues for participation that are also transparent, equitable and accountable to wider public interests is an important first step in fostering more socially just urban environments.

Gentrification often results in decreases in economic and ethnic diversity within urban communities, as well as inter-neighborhood isolation and inequality. Keeping gentrified neighborhoods socially and economically diverse, scholars argue, remains key to curbing unrest (Squires 1989; Walks & Maaranen 2008). We have argued that global neoliberal policies and practices increasingly drive the nature of urban regeneration, accelerating the vulnerability of and displacement of the economically disadvantaged. Concerns about environmental sustainability, the provision and consumption of services, and the changing nature of work have each contributed to shifting patterns of urban regeneration. Ideological assumptions, coupled with social and political interests remain the motivating force behind revitalization projects, which often elevate economic success over the best interests of individuals and communities. In pursuit of a more Just City model of urban life, participatory practices must be augmented by a political commitment to foster more equitable and affordable urban communities. There is a need for new mechanisms to represent the interests of the public, particularly the economically disadvantaged, so as to counter the general trend of growing social exclusion, dislocation and disenfranchisement in the North American city.

## References

August, M. (2014) "Challenging the Rhetoric of Stigmatization: The Benefits of Concentrated Poverty in Toronto's Regent Park", *Environment and Planning*, 46: 1317–1333.

August, M., and Walks, A. (2012) "From Social Mix to Political Marginalization? The Redevelopment of Toronto's Public Housing and the Dilution of Tenant Organizational Power", In G. Bridge, T. Butler, L. Lees, and T. Slater (eds.), *Mixed Communities: Gentrification by Stealth?* Bristol: The Policy Press. Pp. 273–298.

Bornstein, L., and Leetmaa, K. (2015) "Moving beyond Indignation: Stakeholder Tactics, Legal Tools and Community Benefits in Large-Scale Redevelopment Projects", *Oñati Socio-Legal Series*, 5: 29–50.

Bowles, S., and Gintis, H. (1986) *Democracy and Capitalism: Property, Community, and Contradictions of Modern Social Thought*. New York, NY: Basic Books.

Bridge, G., Butler, T., and Lees, L. 2012. *Mixed Communities: Gentrification by Stealth?* Bristol, UK: The Policy Press.

Chesnay, C., Bellot, C., and Sylvestre, M. (2013) "Taming Disorderly People One Ticket at a Time: The Penalization of Homelessness in Ontario and British Columbia", *The Canadian Journal of Criminology and Criminal Justice*, 55(2): 161–185.

DeFilippis, J. (2004) *Unmaking Goliath*. New York: Routledge.

DeFilippis, J., and Wyly, E. (2008) "Running to Stand Still: Through the Looking Glass with Federally-Subsidized Housing in New York City", *Urban Affairs Review*, 43(6): 777–816.

Dryzek. J. (1996) *Democracy in Capitalist Times: Ideals, Limits, and Struggles*. Oxford, UK: Oxford University Press.

Eisen, J.B. (2009) "Brownfields Development: From Individual Sites to Smart Growth", *Environmental Law Reporter: News and Analysis*, 39(4): 10285–10290.

Fainstein, S. (2010) *The Just City*. Ithaca, NY: Cornell University Press.

Hackworth, J. (2007) *The Neoliberal City: Governance, Ideology, and Development in American Urbansim*. Ithaca, NY: Cornell University Press.

Hardt, M., and Negri, A. (2004) *Multitude: War and Democracy in the Age of Empire*. New York, NY: Penguin.

James, R.K. (2010) "From 'Slum Clearance' to 'Revitalisation': Planning, Expertise and Moral Regulation in Toronto's Regent Park", *Planning Perspectives*, 25: 69–86.

Jonas, A.E.G., and McCarthy, L. (2010) "Redevelopment at All Costs? A Critical Review and Examination of the American Model of Urban Management and Regeneration", In J. Diamond, J. Liddle, A. Southern, and P. Osei (eds.), *Urban Regeneration Management: International Perspectives*. New York, NY: Routledge. Pp. 31–62.

Kohn, M. (2013) "Privatization and Protest: Occupy Wall Street, Occupy Toronto, and the Occupation of Public Space in a Democracy", *Perspectives on Politics*, 11: 99–110.

Laakso, J. (2013) "Flawed Policy Assumptions and HOPE VI", *Journal of Poverty*, 17(1): 29–46.

Leitner, H., Peck, J., and Sheppard, E.S. (2007) *Contesting Neoliberalism: Urban Frontiers*. New York, NY: Guildford Press.

Madanipour, A. (2010) *Whose Public Space? International Cases in Urban Design and Development*. New York, NY: Routledge.

McCarthy, L. (2009) "Off the Mark? Efficiency in Targeting the Most Marketable Sites Rather Than Equity in Public Assistance for Brownfield Redevelopment", *Economic Development Quarterly*, 23(3): 211–228.

O'Grady, B., Gaetz, S., and Buccieri, K. (2013) "Tickets . . . and More Tickets: A Case Study of the Enforcement of the Ontario Safe Streets Act", *Canadian Public Policy*, 39(4): 541–558.

Orueta, F.D., and Fainstein, S. (2008) "The New Mega-Projects: Genesis and Impacts", *International Journal of Urban and Regional Research*, 32(4): 759–767.

Pollard, J.S. (2004) "From Industrial District to Urban Village? Manufacturing, Money and Consumption in Birmingham's Jewellery Quarter", *Urban Studies*, 41(1): 173–193.

Porter, L., and Shaw, K. (2009) *Whose Urban Renaissance? An International Comparison of Urban Regeneration Strategies*. New York, NY: Routledge.

Purcell, M. (2008) *Recapturing Democracy: Neoliberalization and the Struggle for Alternative Urban Futures*. New York, NY: Routledge.

Rerat, P., Soderstorm, O., and Piguet, E. (2010) "New Forms of Gentrification: Issues and Debates", *Population, Space and Place*, 16(5): 335–343.

Slater, T. (2006) "The Eviction of Critical Perspectives from Gentrification Research", *International Journal of Urban and Regional Research*, 30: 737–757.

Squires, G. (1989) *Unequal Partnerships: The Political Economy of Urban Redevelopment in Postwar America*. New Brunswick, NJ: Rutgers University Press.

Walks, A., and Maaranen, R. (2008) "From Gentrification to Social Mix, or Social Polarization?: Testing the Claims in Large Canadian Cities", *Urban Geography*, 29(4): 293–326.

# Index